SPIRIT OF PLACE

in Finistère

WENDY MEWES

with illustrations by Lynette Hardwick

Spirit of Place
in Finistère
published by Red Dog Books
ISBN 978-0-9935815-2-6

© Wendy Mewes 2016

British Library Cataloguing-in-Publication Data
A catalogue record for this book is available from the British Library

Red Dog Books is based in Somerset and in Brittany.
Enquiries should be addressed to the editorial office at
Red Dog Books, 29690 Berrien, France.

email: reddogbooks@orange.fr

www.reddogbooks.com

Printed by imprintdigital.net

For Jeanne Le Bourgeois
my true friend

ACKNOWLEDGEMENTS

Thanks to Lynette Hardwick for her
meticulous illustrations
and to Yves Marhic for his translation of the
French edition of this book

About the author

Wendy Mewes has lived in Finistère for many years. She is the author of numerous books about Brittany, and her articles have appeared widely in the UK press. In France she has been filmed for TV and contributed to radio broadcasts on historical subjects.

Her extensive work to promote Breton history and culture to English-speaking visitors and residents through walks, talks, courses and guided visits began when she founded Brittany Walks in 2004. She now concentrates on walking and landscape writing.

She is a member of the Society of Authors and the Association des Écrivains bretons.

For more information:
website   wendymewes.com
blog   wendymewes.blogspot.com

Author's Note

The texts LAYERS, COAST and PLACE NAMES formed part of an exhibition on the landscape of Brittany at L'Autre Rive, Berrien in 2015.

The text OUESSANT has been adapted from my book *Brittany, a cultural history*, published by Signal Books, Oxford in 2014 as part of their Landscapes of the Imagination series.
(See another extract, page 130)

CONTENTS

INTRODUCTION

There are certain small corners of Finistère that have lingered in my imagination since first acquaintance and entered my inner world on some significant level. I wanted to explore through the medium of 'place writing' their distinct personalities and atmospheric qualities, to touch what separates them from the hundreds of other beautiful spots in the same area.

It is quite deliberate that few individual people are named in this book, which is about elemental landscape, although historical detail has an inevitable part to play. Places are shaped by the actions of man, with hardly a metre untouched by human hand at some point in history, but it is usually the ordinary unnamed who have through their labour fashioned the appearance of the countryside today.

There are those places, however, that seem to take their character, the *genius loci*, from another source, from nature itself. Here I have tried to describe the elements and qualities that create distinctive places, and the emotional connections they stimulate within us. I believe that there is a point beyond accepted notions of beauty and traditional cultural filters where each individual can relate on an entirely different and more profound level with their own special places.

LAYERS

Landscape lies in layers of vision and perception.

Tweaking, cosseting, coercing nature into forms
and patterns of exploitation, man made landscape.
Marked by cruel struggle of the farmer, the twisted
back of the stone-cutter, the fierce joy of the hunter
and the body count of the waves.

Earth, like a lover, shares pain and satisfaction.

There's too much outside looking in these days.
Appearance is all, better if bizarre or extreme.
Swift glance. Click and go.
Where is that lost intimacy of living with the land?

Landscape in Brittany is slow and subtle.
Those suffering from terminal quickness need
long-stay respite care here.
To live on a scale that matches man to nature.
To burrow down into the layers of land and
its language.
Emotional alignment.

This requires old gone skills, skills hard to master.
Stillness, silence, self-less awareness.

Make a start.
Touch the rock, taste the berry and the nut,
hear the curlew cry,
scent out the line where salt meets sweet on the tide,
look into the mirror of landscape.
Experience. Now is all.

SPIRIT OF PLACE

When we look into the mirror of landscape we see initially a reflection of ourselves: our own emotions, preferences and cultural references applied to the natural world. But it is possible to go further, to see through the looking-glass and engage with the essence of place.

Some places are outstanding and memorable by virtue of the unique atmosphere they emanate. Some palpable presence speaks of individual identity, a kind of personality of place. On an immediate level, we are often attracted by the striking form of a landscape feature, or the harmonious blend of nature and man-made structure, but only in certain rare spots can an enduring spirit be found, a distinctive energy that has imbued the locale with character. Recognition of this may come from an impression of duration and continuity, the sense of a watchful guardian in position through aeons. These special places seem separated from unremarkable surroundings by invisible boundaries that we feel rather than see. A picturesque scene of great natural beauty is a different thing from a place where some discrete *genius loci* dwells. The heart of our experience of such places is connection.

In earlier times people saw the landscape more functionally than today, when many have forgotten or never known how things are made and produced. Then landscape was livelihood. There existed nevertheless a strong semi-poetic vision of the dynamism of locality which lingers in popular song, place-names and legends centred on place. The particular intimacy forged by usage and inter-dependence may no longer be accessible for most of us, but in our time, with its luxury of leisure and increasingly unsteady sense of anchorage, it is yet possible to forge a different relationship with the land and come closer to the secrets of our shared existence.

The landscape is a sponge for emotions, the great soakaway of human experience. We bring our woes and stresses to nature and lay them down at the feet of the sea or on a lonely mountain top or beside a quiet forest pool. Often we seek nature's company simply because it demands and expects nothing from us, giving temporary release from inner burdens or the opportunity to ponder issues in the comfortable airy freedom of the outdoors. The search for peace and quiet is a strong factor in our need for landscape, balm for the human individual who is so rarely physically alone and in silence in modern life. We also respond deeply to the expansion of our vitality into open space and the basic practice of walking, man's most natural pace, which puts us back into a lost rhythmic relationship with the detail of landscape.

Some places commemorate historical events, or contain the relic of religious ardour or may have been the scene of our own significant personal history, a spot shared with someone loved. Residual human energy lingers, even over thousands of years. Why not? If human experience is valuable, it surely lasts. We feel its cumulative accretion in the singular atmosphere of places like churches or battle sites. But the simple standing-stone placed by unknown hands beside a spring on a little visited site or a remote forest glade can be as spiritually animated as the greatest cathedral in the land. The explanation lies in something outside us and our emotions.

Our first layer of response to landscape is usually visual, especially if the object is striking enough: the remarkable shape and size of trees and rocks draws attention, the power of tidal movement, a colour palette that, despite its richness, soothes the eye. But where the spirit of place prevails, a more sensory perception emerges, as straightforward as touching the fabric of stone or listening to the music of water, as indefinable as intuiting earth's energy, 'a feeling in the air', a sense of being in a place apart.

Cultural reference is another strong perceptive force in reaction to the landscape, a force that both binds and separates us from nature. It is the role of the formalized imagination, developed at a societal level over great stretches of time with universal themes expressed through legends and folktales. It is like a gauzy curtain through which we can see outlines, shadows and symbols that provoke long memories of human experience.

Emotional connection is crucial to our involvement with the land, but we can move beyond our own immediate moods, beyond historical association and cultural traditions to a simpler, more instinctive exchange. It happens not when we are deliberately looking for solace, concealment, comfort or inspiration from nature, but when we open ourselves to the stillness of calm isolation and allow the undemanding atmosphere to lay aside our own selves and unfurl our receptiveness. Without expectation and with heightened consciousness we can go beyond the veil of outer appearance into an authentic communication with the spirit of place itself.

This is the higher stage, the advanced relationship with the *anima loci* which spurs our capacity to absorb the essence of another entity outside our conventional range, blurring the boundaries between reason and intuition. Direct communication with the spirit of place is an experience of true connection, something shared, the deep awareness that landscape is speaking to us of itself - which is also ourselves. We are united in life, death and rebirth. The aridity of modern life that cuts us off from the earth falls away, to be replaced by a deeply desired intimacy. We remember and experience in our mind and body that we are made of the same stuff as the earth. We are no longer separate. We belong.

BARNENEZ

Imposition. The cairn of Barnenez may be the oldest structure in Europe, the first creation of landscape, placing man's mark on the environment. The prominent situation, yet below the highest ground, reflects a gesture of assimilation rather than dominance. It's both a monument of the dead, and a monument of living aspiration and achievement.

The huge funerary structure, orientated east/west, contains eleven tombs, built in two phases – the first five about 4600BC - separated by a thousand years, twice enfolded in the land. Eleven doorways, eleven passages and eleven burial chambers: a terrace of dead neighbours, a defunct community echoing the values and social continuity of its creators. It is also an abiding memorial, although those responsible could scarcely have anticipated the endurance of their project. The cairn of Barnenez changed the colour of the landscape.

This monument, once 80m long and 30m wide, is as powerfully impressive now as one imagines was the original intention. Local dolerite formed the first phase, with granite from the nearby Île Stérec used for the later extension, perhaps a conscious separation of material. The dry-stone work of the overall structure, a huge carapace of graded smaller stones protecting the graves, is remarkable for its time, and the actual tombs show a range of techniques from chambers shaped by stone slabs to more sophisticated *tholos*-style circular roofs. The architectural abilities and degree of organization demonstrated rather give the lie to the concept of primitive prehistoric society.

The scale and prominence of the monument were in themselves a statement of possession and confidence, an artistic definition of the degree of security generated by the start of settlement and ownership. If our impression is instinctively formed by the enormously solid presence of Barnenez today, the cairn also expresses a process of creation and evolution. It is a veritable happening of stone, from the moving of material to the site to renewal of use over a long period of time, as finds from the Bronze Age and the medieval period indicate.

It represents more than prehistoric perceptions of death and the potential of a society able to organize work on this scale. The triumph of technological progress and artistic development must have meant a lot to the living, extending their skills and knowledge though a learning process of method and form, teaching them the wider potential of stone and the rewards of studying the lie of the land. This process of ambition and of achievement characterizes the true quality of experience that enhances social assurance and human satisfaction.

If the dead were provided in their grave-goods with the means of a metaphysical journey, their actual passing from the landscape was replaced by the monument which the survivors set down as a marker. This is ours. The bones of our ancestors are the roots we have fashioned through planting seeds. We know this place and what can be done here. This is a symbol of our productivity. We have learnt how to fix our impression on the landscape.

The dead have no further needs but they leave the imprint of authority, lend an authenticity that will secure the future. They pioneered the possession of land, the concept of ownership and partnership between man and nature. It was a way found through exploration. So there is a transmission of intention from generation to generation and the exceptional mass of the cairn reflects the solidity of attainment on the land, forming a lasting bond with the earth.

The landscape is much changed, as always where the littoral is concerned. The waves of the Bay of Morlaix now lap at the base of Barnenez's prominence, and the tide cuts off the tongue of land of Île Stérec. It was quite a different story then. A wide plain, split by the river, separated low ranges of hills, towards what is now Locquenolé and the promontory of Carantec. The sea was in abeyance, not an integrated part of the physical conception of the monument, although maritime traffic and transport were already commonplace in the Neolithic world.

This harmonious imposition fits the terrain, the latter phase on lower land tiered by stepped buttressing, melding itself to the natural lines of the hill. It may have been shaped to mirror the perception of a tiered cosmos, the stratification of sky, earth and below, with passage tombs the horizontal wells that reach inside, paths between life and death. Or even a vast vessel poised for the western seas where spirits of the dead came to rest. Through the earth, under the stone, along the passage. It is one of the first ever assertions of the relationship between natural landscape and built landscape.

The cultivation of the land that characterizes the Neolithic brought man into quite a different relationship with his environment, from transient grazing to growing seeds to putting down roots. Care and husbandry of resources led to the intimacy with the land that precedes a concept of belonging and then ownership. Commitment to a specific section of earth means not only the labour needed to rotate crops and manage animals, but the imperative of defence, to be prepared to fight for what has been accomplished and refuse to yield the benefits to outsiders. It is also salutary to advertise presence and occupation in peace time, to set out the stall of primitive property rights by marking territory as an animal would. In this sense Barnenez offers a powerful statement of settlement articulated in stone: this land is of us, our ancestors and our descendants.

The biggest threat to the monument's survival came from the modern world. In the 1960s a developer began systematic destruction for the useful building stone when a new road was being laid nearby to meet the demands of tourists on the coast of the Bay of Morlaix. A second cairn nearby was completely destroyed. Fortunately the extremity of his actions highlighted the significance of the site and its vulnerability, leading to classification of historic importance, despite the considerable damage already inflicted.

To pass a few hours in silent companionship with the mortal structure of Barnenez is to touch that awareness that initiated the dynamic connection between man and land. It is the first expression of the potential intimacy of natural and built landscape, even if today it is the character of the cairn itself that remains, real and emphatic, unlike the unknown individuals it housed whose bones have long leeched away into the earth. A powerful but curiously uplifting *memento mori*, it is also a reminder of our own roots in the landscape as we touch base with one of humankind's earliest cultural endeavours.

We have come so far and so fast from that time, so disconnected from the cohesive values of small society, but the development of monuments springs still from similar motives of advertisement and commemoration. The cairn's setting is a reminder that what we share and what unites us with our Neolithic forebears is the interaction with the elements. There is still no way of mastering them, even if we are more capable of storing and using or abusing the resources of the earth. We are still under the same rain.

TUCHENN GADOR

Absorption. Sun ricochets off pellucid points embedded in the muddy grey-brown of the rock where I sit. A myriad of quartz crystals stamped over the surface, hard, pure shards glinting and glimmering, bright as snow, rough as bristles. This lofty outcrop is shaped like a group of haggard old men at a bar: weather-beaten faces, tortuous limbs desiccated by time. A few leeward perches offer protection from the slash of the unfettered north-west wind. It's February, and this is the place for weather-watchers, a seat in the gods to witness a play of sudden appearances and disappearing acts against a backdrop of apocalyptic clouds.

Before me, heights circle a vast sodden depression, with a swathe of woods sealing the scene to the east. A diagonal stretch of hills defines the southern boundary of the Monts d'Arrée, and beyond Roc'h Kleguer (the 'rocky rock'), fluid contours on the far horizon redraw the low line of the Montagnes noires, like a dense grey wave. The boundless sweep of sky encompasses a billowing mass, coloured from deep slate to puffs of white like speech-bubbles. Showers wet the high forest, a sea of mist obscures the anchorage of the communications mast on top of the northern range, black edges of moving rain pass over the background and from the south-west, sunshine chases huge shadows across the levels.

All this at one time. Below, nature is stripped to the bone: ragged ridges of stone, soft curves of heath and a great sunken bowl of marsh. The landscape is inauspicious, inhospitable and unpredictable as the weather. Superimposed is the hand of man: a road, a reservoir, a hill-top chapel. Setting for ancient rites, hard labour, dark tales. An unusual place. Where else can you see a nuclear power station and a Neolithic alignment in one single view?

All rock is remnant. Something which is less than it was. Granite that has gone, in this case, leaving a foundation of *grès or* sandstone, topped here and there by more resistant craggy crests. What we verbalize as a symbol of solidity and endurance, moulded by the metamorphosis of time, is relentlessly eroded under exposure. The Monts d'Arrée are the highest hills in

Brittany, top-spots on the western edge of Europe's landmass. I can just see the culminating point, Roc'h Ruz, to the east, a gnarled pimple of schist on the skin of moor towards Roc'h Trédudon, black dot in the mist. At less than 400m these hills may belie their name in appearance, but they retain an atmospheric vestige of that distant childhood when they were contiguous with the Alps. Here the slow life of stone marches on.

The Breton name for the butte where I'm watching is Tuchenn Gador, Hill of the Throne, a reference to the eponymous protruding rock formation, topping the long back and smooth flank of this eminence rising from the sea of marsh like a becalmed green whale. French map-makers in the 18th century couldn't cope with the outlandish language of the locals for this outlandish spot and marked it Toussaines, a civilising euphony. All Saints could not be less appropriate in this stark yet emblematic environment. My rocky perch is an eyrie for observation of the very heart of Brittany, a seat of power, both nuclear and imaginative.

From here begins a visual journey through landscape immersed in antiquity, a past still sharing its presence alongside modern man's ultimate manipulation of nature. One glance takes in the muted conic and iconic hill of old sun gods, now topped with a lonely chapel of St-Michel, the saint staking his claim for Christian cosmology, a futile quest for domination over the indomitable terrain of primeval deities. On the plateau below, dozens of small raised stones spread over the moor, tracing the wavy line beloved by Neolithic designers at the time when this raw terrain was first stripped and exploited for resource and ritual, first of many losing battles in the misty arena of battling winds and rain. The main road from Morlaix to Quimper, cut from my view below by a bulging roll of wild grass, also snakes around the perimeter below the crests, grandly aping those same sinuous curves.

The fierce struggle replayed over thousands of years has defined the essence of the land, its inhabitants and its stories. In the giant's bowl created by the enclosure of hills lies the great tract of peaty marsh, the Yeun Elez, source of legend and alleged site of an entrance to the Celtic underworld. It is now crossed by wooden walkways in much the same way as early man must have traversed the treacherous shifting surface, today half-obscured by the reservoir of St-Michel, created in 1930 to feed a hydro-electric plant at St-Herbot. This greatly limited the traditional livelihood based on peat-extraction. Struggles between men and their conflicting interests are as apparent in the landscape as that between man and nature.

But the bog persists. A place that holds on to legends and secrets, a blanket of mystery tucked well down at the corners, despite man's preoccupation with functionality. Some time after 5000BC, a creeping layer of sphagnum moss sealed the watery surface of the basin, allowing the *tourbière* to form beneath. Made up of rotted matter, this transformed into a different entity, durable and tenacious. Dead, but alive. Palynology has given us the date and evidence of prehistoric growth on the surrounding slopes, oak, birch, hazel, and traces of wheat from the time of man's first cultivation and search within the earth for sustenance. As the trees were cleared, grasses and their kin, like sorrel, mugwort and ribwort plantain began to claim the territory for themselves, the earliest development of heath or *landes*, ideal grazing land.

Precipitation comes down from the sky and wells back up out of the earth. This is the cradle of rivers as well as legends. The Elez rises just out of my view to the west, its early progress retarded by the flat plain of lost granite that holds up a rapid descent towards the Aulne. This delay allows water to penetrate deep into the acidic soil, where stagnation is a natural state, in contrast to the superficial management of water demonstrated by the reservoir. Immediately behind the ridge of Tuchenn Gador, in a valley wedged between rocky moor and quarry scars, another spring bursts out of the floor, starting spurt of the Elorn which will transform itself into a vast estuary before reaching the Rade de Brest 40 kilometres away.

The marshy waste and heath that dominate the view contrast sharply with a thick wooded coating around the nearby settlement of Botmeur, the cultivated Presqu'ile, sticking out like a sore foot into the lake, and more distant La Feuillée, said to be the highest village in Brittany. Small fields - characteristic of the Monts d'Arrée - are shiny little emerald patches embroidered on the mousey-grey quilt of winter trees and odd knots of evergreens that thrive in poor soil. On the open side of the lake are more spruce, these parcels intrusive, one a great dark square like a Roman army camp, another a line of troops drawn up for battle. Their uniform shapes are out of step with the fluid lines of landscape here. All destined for the chop. On the actual unctuous marshes only a few stunted individuals stand out like scaffolds.

The unpopulated character of this central hub of the Monts d'Arrée is clear from old maps where white space dominates even when the name of every tiny hamlet is writ large. The unfriendly soil held little scope for aristocrats and fine houses. No-one panders to over-lords here: it takes an independence of spirit to survive. Once a large proportion of the inhabitants of

Botmeur and La Feuillée squeezed survival as *pilhaourien*, rag-and-bone men, travelling far afield when their meagre plots could spare the labour. Gruelling effort may be needed to make a living in this terrain, but it is not utter desolation. No-one in this area could afford the luxury of wilderness. Men and women who knew the land on its own terms could work on its level and eke out an existence. A few corners were cut for hay, gorse for bedding and the peat for fuel, before the flooding of the Elez basin. *Blé noir* or sarrasin, the hundred-day miracle crop, not only grows in such infertile earth but nourishes the soil in the process, now as in hardier times.

Primitiveness and unpredictability led to a poor reputation with outsiders, a sense of mystery and unseen dangers, distorted sounds, flickering lights in the darkness, the home of malevolent spirits, a world apart in the remote, inaccessible core of Finistère's landscape. The difficulties of moving around and passing through from the north were used as an argument against the capital of the new department being established at Quimper at the time of the Revolution. In the 19th century there was only a single house on the old road that passed from Brasparts to Plouneour-Menez, twenty kilometres of risk and uncertainty, at the mercy of weather, wolves and worse.

Everything is sucked back into the past by the very nature of the place. Neither bog nor moor is modern. For all their emblematic value of scientific advance, the nuclear power station could well pass for the castle of some grey lord from the distant past, the communications mast for the totem of a giant race. The dangers of this environment are brought out in the old tales, allying legends to their context, holding up a mirror to the landscape. Stories wear the dark face of the earth, echoing travellers' fears of being lost in an abandoned landscape without refuge or comfort.

So Ankou the Grim Reaper stalks the tracks in his clanking cart. A black dog glimpsed through the brume means death. Nocturnal washerwomen call to hapless travellers on the moors at night to help with folding sheets that turn to shrouds which crush their bones and wring out their lives to nothing. The *korrigans*, ugly little imps housed in pre-historic burial places, dance on the moors at night and will invite a passing stranger to join their dance in the round, then never loosen their grip until they've danced the life from him. This is the way to deal with strangers who invade their privacy. There is a Wild West element to the Monts d'Arrée, stories reflecting that outsiders have no business there, that rules are inexpedient and irrelevant to the harsh imperative of living in rough land. The indifference to the world outside is strength not weakness.

The story of the priest who calls on God to turn drunken revellers to stone sums up the polarization of insiders and outsiders. The norms of society are not respected as the merrymakers on the moor refuse to make way for the priest carrying the Holy Sacrament – he should have known better than to cross this heath himself - so they are punished for their sin by petrification. This explanation of the line of stones that make up the Neolithic alignment An Eured Vein, the Stone Wedding Party, is hardly an account in the church's favour. Older powers may be held in respect here, but the god of Catholicism has little place in the Monts d'Arrée, where people have their own way of doing things and it's no concern of theirs if others take exception.

Looking down from above emphasises the ensemble of elements, and the incongruities man has latched onto the land. Only the metal thrust of the communications antenna is significantly higher than where I lean against the rock, and this appears and recedes within layers of mist. The site remains a symbol of the politicization of landscape, object of a bomb attack in 1974, protest against TV and radio broadcasting in French to the detriment of the Breton language. In those days there were two masts and one was brought down by the blast. So too was the assistant director of the site, struck by a heart attack in response to the damage. Breton nationalists claimed responsibility, although the event has already taken on a layer of obfuscation demanded by legends of the Monts d'Arrée.

All narratives become old. The nuclear centre is in course of long dismantlement, a process not without its controversies, and will one day be lost to view. There will be tales of metamorphosis in the future. Memories last here. The very isolation of this area attracted the building of the power station in the early 1960s, a few years before the same distinctive environment was included in the establishment of the natural regional Parc d'Armorique. The theoretical incompatibility of the two ideas proved no deterrent. Emptiness is as emptiness does, after all. Better action than sterility, the argument may go, but nature will always have the last word. It is the greatest of all movers and shakers.

The panorama before me is dominated by the mobility of air, the upper strata of clouds moving steadily from the south-west across the vista like a parade, loftily above the level of the moors, where snapping bites of wind from the north continually break the calm. A buzzard from his high trapeze slices the big sky, swooping like an avenging angel to wreak havoc on the blameless life of voles. Air is the element of the moors, sharp and penetrative, stirring the mental process, swirling without obstruction over the levels, unfurling cerebral patterns. Here is the place for thinking wide thoughts, for opening the mind to possibilities that lie unconsidered in confined spaces. Expansive strides and wide views work on the brain, tricking out a longer thread, unravelling the matted worries that beset life in houses.

Moor holds on to things just like the bogs below. Gorse, broom and heather thrive, lending perennial colour to the scene. The bleached winter moor-grass, clinging on to an echo of pale sunlight in its soft biscuit hue, bends, and brittle ferns crinkle with the breezes, rippling and blending, tough and resilient like all inhabitants of this harsh world. Here the earth is always moving, changing. The land is hard and soft by degrees, water everywhere, even on the higher ground, lurking just below the surface of stone tracks, giving underfoot for a springy step. It is a greedy, retentive place, sucking and suckering, pulling back and down, grasping a bit of everything that passes across its deceptive surfaces, retaining experience in a wet web. Down below, earth and water play out their love-affair beneath the prickly sheets of vegetation. Each time I walk these moors it is hand in hand with old ideas imprinted on the land.

To identify with the singular character of the Monts d'Arrée is today a form of resistance to the globalization that reduces life to sameness and predictability. It is not a comfortable place. It feels like something left behind from another time, vestige of a past more ancient than we can imagine. Not even the most sophisticated of man's scientific achievements has really touched on that. Here landscape tells its own tale in its own language, the story of rock declining and water imbibing. Here the separation between reality and imagination is really not so great. All is absorption. The spirit of this place is tenacious, private but alive.

The battle of the elements is finally won by rain, drawing in the view to a murky mass, settling on my shoulders as I descend the stony path into the mist.

HUELGOAT

Regeneration. I live on the edge of a forest, at the point of stepping into a discrete world. It holds that special edgy energy, defensive and anticipatory. Forest's realm is segregated by very visible, natural boundaries, giving the process of entry a ritual sense of moving from one state to another. Wooden walls and a green roof raised on many pillars create shape and structure for the forest at large, yielding an atmosphere of enclosure and containment. A mass of trees like this is a veritable community, like any town or village, with all the issues of shared resources, inter-dependence and rivalries that involves. Forest is as complex and intricate as any relationships between people.

At human scale, to be within forest is anything but a clear-cut experience. The sphere of vision is curtailed by foliage, trunks and branches, perspective distorted by winding paths. Sounds change according to the moisture in the air and the breath of wind on the trees. With separation from the guiding point of sun or stars, it is a natural place of disorientation, which has engendered two strong cultural images: losing one's way and identity-swapping, taking on a new persona within the forest limits.

My forest is a hilly one, riven into a landscape dominated by broken granite, tremendous boulders dotting the oak and beech clad slopes. Trees sprout from the very rock, in a relationship of faith. In winter, among a mass of grey skeletons, evergreens stand out, not in rigid phalanx but irregular clumps here and there, dark bands of knights surviving in a last stand to defend the hill-tops. Every ripple of contour nurtures a fall of stream. The highs and lows of terrain give plunging torrents to swell the river-beds in frequent times of rich rainfall. The crash and curl of the water adds to the drama, for there is always a touch of theatre in forest, a sense of unfolding scenes.

This forest is littered by rocks, perched like sentries on the high ridges, dramatically tumbled down a narrow river valley, or polished by forceful streams which rub them smooth, shaped into the emptiness of caves and tunnels, harbouring wedges of damp old air in their impenetrable folds. The Chaos at the head of the Argent valley is the result of an old war between fire and earth, magma swelling and cooling over an unimaginable period of time and eroding, worn and fissured, to split and buff into boulders that eventually succumb to a random tumbling. The resulting mountains of misshapen rocks balance in a vast carapace above the deep channel of the river, driving the force of life below, unseen like a subterranean engine. So water underpins chaos, contributing to the forest's sense of unseen powers and movement. Forest is potent.

Two rocks stand out by size and shape and isolation from the others around them. The Mushroom looks exactly that, a granite *chanterelle* worthy of a giant's appetite. The Trembling Rock is a massive almost rectangular slab, estimated to weigh more than 100 tons and yet capable of a slight shiver if touched in the right spot. Physics in a magic cloak. The surrounding slopes are covered in other lumps of stone, many bearing strange gashes like bodies on a battlefield, lines of small rectangular holes or smoothed edges that look unnatural. These are wounds from stone-cutting tools, in what was once a working quarry, and the disappearance of so much granite in the vicinity is accounted for by this important 19th century industry. The local clear grey version was much in demand for building work, and its exploitation almost oversaw the destruction of the very Chaos itself.

But the time when the quarry thrived also saw a burgeoning interest in Bretonness, in the wonders of a landscape steeped in the legend that characterized its oral Celtic culture. Such sites were to become intrinsic in the concept of Breton identity. As the region's population became more mobile with the spread of railways, the concept of holidays and leisure pursuits, exploration of previously isolated spots away from the better-known coastal regions became possible. The unusual and exotic in a setting of natural beauty had a special allure. Slowly the balance between industry and tourism as a means of supporting the local economy began to shift, and forest – that place of transformative powers – began a change of persona from utilitarian to picturesque.

In the defence of Chaos, various champions stepped forward as the expanding activities of the quarrymen endangered the most compelling of the area's natural attributes. There were references to 'acts of vandalism', whilst eminent literary figures like Anatole Le Braz and Victor Ségalen wrung their hands over the potential scale of loss. The President of the Touring Club de France sent a strong letter to the Prefect of Finistère, and combined with the recently formed *Societé pour la protection des paysages de France,* pressured local authorities to protect and preserve that part of the forest. This was eventually achieved by purchase of the Bois de Saoulec in 1903 and the threat of destruction became limited to the heavy footfall of future visitors.

There are after all different ways of exploiting and corrupting the landscape. The spectacular nature of the Chaos is enough to ensure legendary add-ons. The wild primitivism and sheer size of the rocks makes an obvious association with giants. Two unoriginal foundation legends: a fight between the giants of two villages on either side of the forest led to stone-throwing, the shortfall ending up in a sprawl along the deep Argent valley, or a punitive measure taken by Hok Bras against the inhabitants who fed him meagre gruel. When others in the richer plain to the north offered creamy porridge he obligingly uprooted their rocks and hurled them back to the scene of his displeasure. The morality of mocking poverty – o those giants, symbols of pre-human barbarity!

Feebler invention dominates the Chaos today. A sign boasts: *Ménage de la Vièrge*, the Virgin's household utensils. The visitor is required to discern in the stupendous variety of the rocks, the forms of a cauldron, a bed, a cradle for the Son of God. The only mysteries the Catholic Church appreciated were those within their own control. This apparently harmless attempt to control and focus reaction, hits directly at the pagan appearance of the site and the nature of chaos itself, striving to replace the powerful with the banal and to trivialize the strange power of this so very un-Christian lithic playground.

Forest has an intimate connection with death. The occasional echo of gunfire during the hunting season is an everyday reality in this home of deer, wild boar, badgers, foxes and enough birds for a medieval banquet. It is a hiding place, a lick-wound sort of place, but the protection of cover attracts both prey and aggressor.

Man's instinct for killing haunts the forest in another form. Along the path labelled Allée Violette, named in French fashion for the engineer who created it, but by romantic Chinese whisper often transformed into the Avenue of Violets, is a murder scene, of the type that has widely scarred the Breton countryside. Here three young locals were shot by the Germans during the war. This is far removed from Inspector Barnaby or even the legendary dangers of Babes in the Wood. They represent the great number who, with the desperate nonchalance of youth, took action to resist enemy occupation until such bitter ends as a blanket of dirt and leaves on a wooded slope. The bodies of Pierre Ruelen, Jean Volant and Emile Bérthou lay undiscovered on a steep hillside above the river until long after the war had ended. Whenever I hear the explosion of a hunter's gun echoing through the trees I think of falling limbs with human faces. Their memory is perpetuated: a stele in local granite high above easy view contains the detail, a simple plaque by the well-walked path recording the basic fact of short lives and precipitate death. The latter is often honoured by flowers. The hushed breath of the forest contains those young men's future, those unlived courses imagined with a sylvan sheen, celebrated by a perpetual obituary of birdsong.

Forest holds you in. Up the valley of the stream with no name, folds of trees soon curtain the steep valley slopes, cutting off any sense of a world beyond. Evergreens with mossy lower branches still intact offer a series of giant green turnstiles between an uphill track and the river, which is reduced to throaty rumblings with each passage under massive rocks.

These granite hillsides lend themselves to wells of blackness between the massive stones. A cave high up above the path exudes the mystery of darkness and potential danger. The granite formation shows its usual pattern of wear, the vertical and horizontal fissures that hint at some chaotic tumbling in a future too far to contemplate. Left to the imagination, it should be home to dragons, serpents or a lone black bear, but a sign below reads 'Grotte d'Artus', directing the visitor away from personal observation towards received culture and the ubiquitous King Arthur, a more alluring draw for visitors. Nature's efforts are too often not enough for man, who likes his landscape securely self-referential. Cave offers both shelter and prospect, an important combination in the ancient world, but even genuine mind-expanding realities like palaeolithic man enjoying a protected space, decorating the walls with primitive art and knapping flint in the entrance cannot compete with potential Celticism.

Pressing on uphill, the river to the right is noisy when forcing a way down the narrow channel past obstructions, limpid where the bed runs flat. Large grey boulders in a shallow holding of water beyond a small cascade attract the name of Wild Boar's Pool. It would be a natural place for the wild pigs to drink, but there are bizarre stories to explain an acceptably prosaic name. Further upstream the water is levelly calm, its clarity illuminated by the yellow granite sand in the bed. The boulders are sparser here. One has a fine Mohiccan style of grassy hair, another a green crew-cut. At stream level there is quiet containment at the deep heart of the valley.

By contrast, the western flank rises ever more sharply, increasingly wild, increasingly steep and pitted with boulders or the debris of fallen trees. The seemingly unattainable height is daunting; unsurprisingly a position destined for defence, allegedly the last bulwark for Celtic locals against Roman forces. The path angles away from the water to rise, fall and rise across small ridges of rock well below the summit. This produces one of the most beautiful scenes in the forest: almost an avenue, opened up by clearance, enclosing a close-packed stand of slender beeches, sloping down gently toward the stream, topped out in the canopy by one or two pines with their red reptilian bark. At ground level, the dead bodies of trees lying at random, bound in acid-green moss, like a game of giant's fiddlesticks, are potent symbols of the resurrection that is forest's speciality. Within these trunks are fertile sources of new life, a prolific underworld of fungal spores and beetles. If forest has a close acquaintance with death, it also knows how to live again. Its rhythm is regeneration. Within the dark cave, within the fallen tree lies life.

The pinnacle of the forest was once an Iron Age camp - a site excavated by Sir Mortimer Wheeler in 1938 - defended against a Roman foe by the local tribe of the Osismes. Iron Age defence of the precipitous slope was reinforced by a *murus Gallicus*, a Celtic speciality of stepped security formed by tree-trunks laid in solid cross-pattern, joined by nails or spiked joints, filled with rubble and faced with stones. The felled trees opened the perspective necessary for defence.

Once up and inside the old rampart ditches, marked to the north by a medieval *motte*, the plateau is gently rounded, retaining today an open grassy area where trees have been cleared, echoes of before and after forest. The old wells that made surviving siege a reasonable prospect can still be seen inside their modern wooden shelter, not far from the natural massive granite barrier used, together with constructed earth banks, to defend an inner area of the camp, large enough to house many people and animals.

This whole area of the forest is filled with a different atmosphere, enticing, intense, deceptive. Maybe it is fraught with that final battle of the Celts, some lingering energy of the hide and seek of conflict. On a few occasions, figures have flashed into my vision and then dissolved into nothing behind trees or rocks, as if the camp is still peopled by a group living in the unworld of shadows. There is an element of alternative reality here, another dimension of life hidden from clear vision. Of course, they could just be unobtrusive mushroom-pickers, but these half-sightings seem reflective of the essence of forest.

To pass through forest is a veritable journey: it is passage not destination. The camp retains a strong sense of that transient character. This forest is for hiding and concealing, a place where secrets are kept and things out of the ordinary can be concealed. Always there's a feeling of things happening just out of view, behind boulders, among the trees: a disconcerting sense of disorientation and blurred boundaries. It is theatre for sound and sight, backed by the scenery of transformation, an enclosed world lending itself to imaginative play, to change and disruption, pretence and shape-shifting. The shadow is glimpsed whilst the substance eludes us. We sense the movement but do not see the thing that moves. Forest is naturally evanescent.

I pass from the town centre to the southern forest by the canal, cut in the 1770s to take water from lake to mine, more than 5 kilometres away. An earlier attempt, skewed off from the Argent had proved unfit for purpose. The upper canal path is much better known. This still flows and its tiny towpath offers the greenest of routes out to the old mine near Locmaria-Berrien. The moist air and enclosed atmosphere has produced a strangely ethereal realm, far from the weight of legend, where moss gleams phosphorescent on every rock and tree, causing the forest to glow as light fades. Streams cut down across the canal, emanating from steep narrow valleys that then open out roundly in the hillside above, like spoons.

Below the little pumping station I turn back along the lower path of the original canal. Water sprays my legs as I precariously cross slippery tree-trunks over the cascade, which drops to the hydro-electric station far below. The refreshingly lonely trail then traces the lie of the land, following the mostly dry canal bed painstakingly cut into a narrow ledge winding along the steep hillside, the land falling away vertiginously to the right. In places it feels like edging along the window-sill of a tree-scraper. Here there is a powerful sense of the tiered landscape, sliced into layers by human engineering. This route is wilder than other paths: broken branches lie all around, holly trees spread across the channel, weed chokes the pools where streams meander on their path down to the Argent.

The canal ends beneath the height of another medieval *motte*, crowned by a stand of beautiful beeches and supported by the dramatic stack of rock that disappears from view into the earth and rises above it in an overhang above the chasm into which the Argent pounds relentlessly. The scene is veritable *coup de theatre*, the ultimate drama of the forest. Before the river can emerge further down the valley in a wide boulder-strewn bed that offers some of the most beautiful scenes in Brittany, it must pass the ordeal of the Gouffre, a cascade that plunges with a roar into a rocky well of fathomless darkness where it is lost but for the echo of a groan in some subterranean hell of another age.

One of the most elaborated Breton legends is tied to this spot. Here Dahut's servants carelessly tossed the bodies of her discarded lovers after a night of service to her voracious sexual appetite. This 'ruthless siren' (Christian version) was daughter of King Gradlon of Quimper. She perished in one form in the waves around Ys in the Bay of Douarnenez according to the local Atlantis legend, only to emerge triumphant (Breton version) as a sea deity, Ahès. By subterranean passages from the coast, Dahut would make her way here to the trees above the torrent and indulge her limitless desires with a procession of unsuspecting unfortunates.

But the height - or so-called Belvedère today - has a more persuasive secret than Dahut's orgies. Here stands a stele in honour of Victor Ségalen, medical man, author, Chinese specialist, extraordinary explorer of the imagination and spokesman of an ephemeral culture dying under the weight of popularism. A marine doctor, born in Brest in 1878, Ségalen spent years in travel to China where he undertook archaeological digs and immersed himself in Chinese art and literature. Returning to Brittany after WWI, he became ill, fading away under the burden of extreme nervous affliction and mysterious degeneration he himself said he could not diagnose.

He came to Huelgoat for a prolonged sojourn of rest, based at the Hotel d'Angleterre in rue Docteur Jacq. Each day he went out into the woods, considerably less managed than today, where to get away from areas recently exploited for quarrying was to plunge into a true sense of forest in all its prolixity and hidden faces. On May 19th 1919, he went out as usual and did not return. A great storm blew over the forest the following morning and still there was no sign of the writer. His wife came from Brest and after a search, discovered his body here in the secret world above the Gouffre, a spot where they had made love previously. He was propped against a tree, an open copy of Hamlet beside him. Death staged? A wound in his heel had bled profusely, enough to shock the feeble body into death, according to the family story. Suicide is another possibility.

I sit against a tree. Instead of Hamlet, I have Ségalen's own *Voyages au pays du réel*, a work of personal significance. Did he die in torpor, resignation or with deliberation, drawing delight from a last view of the perfect world of nature? There is blue sky above the beech canopy. It's a day from Paradise. He may well have felt that there are worse places to end a long and desperate search for beauty, death inside the May forest, a time and place where ugliness ceases to exist.

LEGENDS

Landscape gets the legends it deserves.

In the oral tradition legends are presented as events that actually happened, with named characters (who may have actually existed) and often specific locations. Story-tellers are well aware that the physical setting of the story is of great importance to the audience, the use of real places being a significant connective factor for the credibility of the tale. The typical landscapes of Brittany – forest, moor, shore - are over and over again the backdrop of legend, as well as common features like caves, remarkable trees and megaliths. Local history, a potent source of pride and belonging, is equally about local geography.

Legends are essentially popular tales, stories of the people and for the people, reflecting a life lived close to nature, to the fearsome power of the sea and vagaries of the weather so crucial to an agrarian existence. Megaliths, which we know to be the work of man, are given stories and names like 'Fairies' house' or 'Giant's tomb' because they seemed to come from another age, fantastic structures created when men were physically larger or nature spirits openly had magical powers. Before the development of scientific principles and detailed historical knowledge, stories offered explanations that are too easy for us now to dismiss as irrational or fantastical, but which could have made perfect sense at the time. Such stories are a way of giving a satisfactory sense to one's surroundings, of understanding the context in which our lives are passed.

Legends can also give prestige and renown to local communities. Place names in Brittany are redolent of the past, of people and events preserved over centuries through the memories of generations in a toponym. A place called Folgoët or Folgoat (fool + wood in Breton) or Toul ar Serpent (hole + serpent) require an explanation, and legends may provide it or, on the other hand, stories may be created to furnish one. Inevitably before the days of deductive and geological awareness, stories evolved to answer the questions why and how.

Creation legends are abundant, with primitive explanations of unusual landscape features. The famous granite Chaos of Huelgoat is a natural geological phenomenon, emanating from the movement of igneous rock over millions of years, but it appears extraordinary even in our modern mechanized world. Giants, those symbols of pre-civilization and untamed landscape, are the culprits in various legends. The debris of stone-throwing by squabbling groups of ogres living nearby is certainly more dramatic and more graphic than accounts of the infinitesimally slow cooling and protrusion of magma, aeons of rainfall and tumbling blocks. Immediacy is a characteristic of story-telling that history and geology cannot match.

Secret spaces must breed secret creatures: the impish *korrigans* beloved in the Breton tradition amongst many other examples of 'little people', like to keep out of human sight. Closely connected with stone, they seek the semi-subterranean shelter of Neolithic burial chambers, the *dolmens* whose remains today so often bring to mind the cultural image of hobbit houses. They merge into the landscape to preserve their privacy. These earth-bound stone-dwellers are also miners, tunnelling beneath the surface, creating secret paths. At night, they can dance on the heath, protected from scrutiny by the isolated setting. We like to imagine some form of recognisable life to fill the empty darkness.

Dangerous terrain breeds stories of threats to life posed by creatures that personify the dark nature of the place. The boggy marsh of the Yeun Elez is patrolled by Ankou, the Grim Reaper, black dogs presaging death, murderous washer-women who twist unwary travellers to death in wringing out their sheets. The remote and uninhabited nature of the terrain gives rise to these elements of strangeness, bred of fear of the unknown hazards of travel in a lonely place. The natural physical context is the source, and gives character to the legends.

We have a self-referential attitude to the landscape. Nature alone is not good enough. Nature must be peopled. Natural places of impressive size or appearance are given heroic, mystical or diabolic association: the Steps of Arthur, Arthur's Cave, Druids' Rock, Devil's Rock. The terms of reference are the easy stimulants of our imagination, our need to create narrative. It's a form of enhancement to link places with famous people, a way of responding to the character of a landscape feature to give it more significance. Links with great or notorious men boost the status of places which reinforces local pride and attracts visitors. Tourism is heavily based on such stories or even behind their genesis.

On the steep side of a river valley in the forest of Huelgoat is a wondrous cave. Huge, dark and atmospheric, it looms high above the path, emanating a sense of mystery and fear. It would make a fitting lair for a dragon or a bear, a cache for buried treasure or hiding place for outlaws. But a large, intrusive sign proclaims this Arthur's Cave (*Grotte d'Artus*, a form of the famous name that smacks of pseudo-medievalism). This, so the story goes, is his resting place where he waits in a state of suspended animation before rising again when his country faces its greatest crisis. The cave itself is magnificent and mysterious. It hardly needs enhancement, but cannot avoid the ubiquitous dial-a-hero Arthur.

The Iron Age fort on top of the same hill is called Arthur's Camp, the suggestion of local hero rallying the population against oppressive invaders, taking a glorious stand for liberty. The talisman of Arthur's name is apparently of greater value and more heroically evocative of struggle against domination than the reality, a historic scene of Celtic resistance against Roman might.

The early religious and political development of Breton society revolved significantly around the foundation of monasteries, which then became a focus for the growth of secular settlements. Legends describing their origins could even be used to endorse the property rights and moral authority of these early religious institutions in later years. The holy men responsible for their establishment were part of the wave of immigration from Britain and Ireland – especially Cornwall and Wales – during the 4th-6th centuries, but of the seven founding saints, only St Samson has historical credentials. It was the story that mattered and came to enshrine the cultural origins of Breton society, preserving man's power over the land in custom and law. Landscape is tied to these beginnings through stories of the Breton saints and sacred geography, a territorial map of religious identification.

ABBAYE DU RELEC

Permeable. The history of Le Relec is written in water. Streams reaching down like crooked fingers from the slopes of the Monts d'Arrée were a powerful attraction, shaping the possibilities of settlement for the Cistercian community which arrived in the 12th century. They were to set up an abbey far from their mother-house at Bégard and far from other major centres of ecclesiastical power in western Brittany. To survive, the monks would have to loosen nature's sodden grasp on the valley of the upper Queffleuth. Here the landscape became a true mark of man's application to his environment.

The site today retains something of the air of enclosure that the original abbey precinct must have lent, located at the centre of a series of spurs like wrinkled stone petals on the northern face of the hills. It is not as sheltered a spot as it looks: wind can surge through valley like a cruel wave, and in frequent times of rainfall, the hillsides transform into a wet slide, disgorging dozens of new streams down to flood the narrow river-bed and its meadows. It was this often saturated swale that the monks had to transform into productive land through hard labour and steady management. The direction and coercion of water would be the benchmark of their success. This control exerted over nature was a physical echo of the early imagery of Brittany's founding saints dominating their environment by clearing the deadwood of paganism and planting seeds of Christianity.

A hidden valley, isolated, recondite, perfect for the privacy of prayer; secluded peace, where God's bounty could be appreciated in the still beauty of nature. These may have been the ideals of hermits and earlier Celtic Christian settlements, but it was nowhere near enough for the Cistercians. It was part of the Rule that the abbey supported itself for food, but here there was potential for much more extensive development, and over the centuries Le Relec was to gain considerable land-holdings and possessions far and wide. Initially the site offered the basic elements to get started: water and wood, stone and soil, all ripe for exploitation in a merging of obligation and aspiration.

There may already have been a religious foundation on the site, if the story is not one created to lend a suitable sanctity to the abbey's later foundation. Tradition places an earlier monastery here, dating from the 6th century, established by St Pol via St Tanguy in the aftermath of a terrible battle in this gaunt landscape at a place called Brank-Alek (willow branch). The fearsomely ruthless warrior lord Conomor, godless since his excommunication for brutality and tyranny, fought and lost his last combat. A triumph for the God-fearers, as his opponents were backed by the soldiers of Childebert, king of the Franks. Subsequent burial of bodies from the field of battle is said to have led to the name Relec from the Latin *reliquiae*, or remains of the dead. There is no evidence for this Celtic religious site with the mysterious name Gerber, which could mean simply 'forest'. This is perhaps not surprising as settlements from such times could have been no more than a collection of wooden huts and a chapel for joint worship, adequate for the simple life with an emphasis on prayer and communion with the divine spirit, whilst practising minimalist self-sufficiency. Viking raiders in the 9th century would have put paid to all that.

The arrival of Cistercian settler monks was a different sort of operation: with expansionist plans as far as making use of the land was concerned, and highly organized. In fact, the community was not even as cut off as all that. Remoteness was conceptual rather than a physical reality. Common sense dictated that markets for surplus produce and essential purchases (like salt) were within relatively easy reach and two former Roman roads from Carhaix, to Morlaix and the Aber Wrac'h, were not far away. The very location of Le Relec is near the boundary where three great areas of medieval Brittany - Trégor, Léon, Cornouaille - met, and the abbey was to possess lands in all of these by gift or purchase. Neither was the monastery a secret from travelling pilgrims who might expect to stay in the large guest-house constructed in later years. One of the local sacred springs, the Fontaine de Notre-Dame, is by the roadside outside the precinct and available to all who passed on their journey.

Nor was Relec isolated enough to escape later violence and destruction in those periods when most of Brittany knew only too well the mayhem and murder of roving military bands: the Wars of Succession in the mid 14th century and the Wars of Religion at the end of the 16th. In 1375 soldiers of the Duke of Lancaster raided the abbey, a severe enough misfortune for the Pope to grant indulgences to those contributing funds for repairs and restoration. This fate was repeated in 1598 by followers of the notorious brigand Guy Eder de la Fontenelle and Royalists in their turn. The monks' carefully husbanded resources would have been as big an attraction as their religious valuables, for by that time the growth of the abbey in wealth and influence had been immense.

Forest clearance had begun in this area as early as the Neolithic period and the crests of schist and quartzite prod up through a coat of heathland, much as the nearby Landes de Cragou today, where fragments of an ancient oak woodland remain near the summit. The removal of many trees to provide wood for projects would hardly have helped water retention on the hillsides. The soil is thin and acidic on slopes of scrubby growth, marshy and boggy in the valley bottom where the little stream of Relec joins the Queffleuth to flow in its fledgling stages before taking on power in confluence with the Brio and veering north towards Morlaix. All of these unruly elements would be worked into productive gardens, pasture and small-holdings.

The built landscape was to be simple, initially using stone easily to hand: blocks of grey granite of Plouneour-Menez for pillars and angle stones, irregular dark schist and lighter quartzite from the nearby slopes of the Monts d'Arrée for the walls of what little remains of the earlier versions of the abbey church. Granite from Huelgoat and Brennilis, suitable for finer work, came later as the site developed, perhaps from lands owned by the abbey. Profitable though this network of possessions and communications may have been, transport by ox and cart was not an easy matter over the rough terrain of the Monts d'Arrée.

The valley's damp tonal notes have never been successfully excluded from the church, which was constructed on the highest ground above the stream. Ground levels have changed as outlines of ancient blocked doorways show, and the building evolved over centuries to gain, in the late 1600s, an elaborate night-stair and a large clock to chide lax monks for late arrival at services. Evidence of the earliest buildings remain in the Romanesque arches and pillars with abstract carvings in the transept crossing. Frequent visitors will be well aware that there has often been as much weather inside the church as out, although recent works have tackled the problem of rising moisture that has beset the abbey over centuries, and the greening stones of the interior are no more. The cleaned walls and pillars of the transept and apsidal chapels echo the purity of the original building, simplicity designed to focus the attention on God, not architectural detail. The nave, truncated by storm damage in 1765, was not rebuilt to its original length, witness the surviving traces of curtailed arches. The Neo-classical façade of 1785 once again made use of the local granite of Plouneour.

Threads of water weave everywhere in this part of the valley. Most evidence for manipulation of these resources dates from the late 18th century when there was much activity in the grounds of the abbey, including the creation or re-working of the *douves*, channels cut around the gardens. A hillside *regarde* (inspection point) sits like a tiny house of fine granite block and thick roof slates on a canalisation of water. It bears the date 1777. From the same period comes the obelisk feature on the monumental fountain in the forecourt, although the actual basin is hundreds of years earlier, and once fed a drinking trough before returning the water to the lake. An aqueduct covered with enormous stone slabs services the fountain, which was used as a washing place by the village women well into the 20th century. In addition there are sacred springs. That of St Bernard – commonly honoured in Cistercian monasteries – is covered by a decorative pyramid in granite and runs down into the stream of Relec. The Fontaine Notre-Dame with its steps and rectangular basin is located on the roadside near the south-eastern corner of the abbey church.

The abiding impression of the site is how it has been adapted to cope with and exploit an excess of humidity resulting from all this aqueous activity. The Upper Queffleuth is fed by three main streams from Le Clos, Lesmenez and Pont ar Moal, all of which have changed their courses over the centuries. These waters were made to serve man with the most basic technology of damming and channelling. The monks needed separate supplies to provide clean drinking water and a sewage system, as well as the irrigation of the vegetable gardens below the church with a sequence of ditches. The control exerted over streams created a kind of moated enclosure which could also function as fortification or flood-device in times of threat, offering the abbey limited protection from raids.

Two lakes for fishing date back at least until the 15th century. These are separated by a causeway, now carrying the road, which was the focal point of an old tale claiming that a horseman was posted here, ready to gallop to Morlaix if the river showed signs of rising to danger level. This is perhaps more a recognition of the changes brought to the valley by the abbey's development than an actual situation. The upper lake once had a hydraulic mill, with some of the stone works that diverted the water still in evidence. It feeds the lower lake, bounded by a dyke planted with trees – today a shady walk - partly retained with blocks of granite. From here two water courses are connected to the remains of the extant mill, one a strong cascade under the bridge, and another regulated by a sluice gate to drive the now rusted turbine. A document of 1542 mentions repairs to the causeway and clearing out lakes. The cadastral map of 1837 shows that the lakes were once bigger, before the encroachment of reeds and marsh.

Exploitation of the rough lands of the Monts d'Arrée also brought innovation. The novel system of the *quevaise*, much discussed in the context of the Cistercians and the Knights of St John in this area, was to attract peasants to settle here, get the upper lands cleared and into production, to the benefit of the abbey and the individuals concerned. A small farm provided shelter for the family and animals, out-buildings for storage and half a hectare of land for subsistence, as well as grazing rights. Such tenure provided greater security than the limited rights of *domaine congéable* as the land could be passed on through the family – but to the youngest, to encourage the older siblings to find their own farms to develop – and not reclaimed by the abbey except in case of abandonment. The scheme encouraged the peasant's allegiance to his own land, allowing a certain sense of freedom and permanence of outlook. This practice probably began early in the abbey's history and was certainly renewed in a wider context in the 16th century as the population rose, new deforestation was required and the cultivation of that survival crop, *blé noir*, began in earnest.

This lean security was bought at the price of considerable hardship. The stark location of those small-holdings excavated at Goënidou on the exposed windy heights above Relec is in marked contrast with the comparative shelter and enclosed sanctuary of the abbey in the valley, although the orderly pattern of development that mirrors the wider management of the abbey's estates is apparent. Approaching from the heights of the Monts d'Arrée today, as pilgrims would once have done, emphasises this contrast, with the abbey tucked into a ruched green blanket below. The harsh textures of the *landes* soften into the lush wooded crevice, where the sombre grey church tower still rears above the trees.

It is unclear from whom if anyone the monks were originally granted their land. The lords of Léon unsurprisingly began to take an interest from their seat in Morlaix as the monks became established, and the dukes of Brittany later became valuable patrons. By gift or purchase Relec's territory expanded to include lands as far apart as Brasparts, Cléder and Guimaec; such possessions inevitably led to legal disputes. Evidence from the processes of St Yves shows the sort of property wrangles that followed, with the abbey accused of land-grabbing at the expense of poor individuals.

We know nothing of the early founder monks themselves, those silent workers peopling and re-shaping the valley. In the late 15th century, the intermittent madness of one abbot brought disturbance and eventually intervention from the Papacy to the order of Relec. Looking back it seems akin to a period of lost innocence. Soon after, the system of commendatory abbots, absentee nominees of the duke of Brittany and later the king of France, brought quarrels and tension with their pursuit of personal profit against the interest of the abbey community and its own work force. It was not even necessary for these nominal heads of staff to set foot on the soil of the Queffleuth valley.

The often bitter power struggles were played out in court cases, where claim and counter-claim were lodged. The secret desires and despair of individuals have left no mark on the tranquillity of the valley. What remains are faint reverberations of the even tenor of their basic work in the exploitation of natural resources, an expression of harmony between man's and nature's efforts. Even if most of the physical exertions fell to the lay brothers. The rhythm of prayer is an echo of the rhythm of manual tasks, closely linked to the changing seasons and hence the natural rhythm of human life. The same regularity and assiduousness were mirrored in the religious order of the monastery and the husbandry that supported its activities. Isolation was transformed through action into connection.

All things change, and the monks' fortunes rose and fell over time. From notions of physical work as prayer, the honourable exploitation of the landscape, the abbey's property-holdings grew and grew into big business, although an inspection of 1600 suggested a period of physical and mental decay. Ultimately it was income and not religious services that kept the abbey functioning, that is to say revenue that could be retained against the greed of the commendatory abbots. Despite disagreeable interludes, there were extensive works on the land - banks, ditches and enclosures - new building and remodelling in the third quarter of the 18th century, with major work to restore the western nave, destroyed in a storm. In 1768 there were twelve monks and revenue was high. However, when the Revolution came and the abbey was confiscated by the state, only four monks and a few horses remained.

What appeals so much to us today about the dour stone church in its watery land? There must be an element of nostalgia for a sense of order and rhythm, an idealized view of man's supposedly civilizing relationship with nature. A pristine world, fuelled by spirituality, untouched by the corruption and violence that has marred our own. A sense that man can do well by the land and do his own nature justice in the process. The site has evolved as landscape always does but the hold of Relec is that despite the differences of time it yet retains so much of the atmosphere of a remote past that we feel must have been a better, simpler time. Even if it wasn't. Dormant vitality lingers, the silence and reflection of a low profile encapsulated in the deep reflective hush into which the valley falls in winter.

The spirit of evolution and renovation has been stirred at Relec in the last few years and an increase in labour and footfall has animated the site with a more active energy that must have been the norm eight hundred years ago. Clearing of the ground has again been an issue, albeit in a localized way with the destruction of a house built near the abbey church in 1913, and the felling of some mighty trees in the same area, simplifying the visual profile of the site. The new openness has been a surprise, an enhanced perspective of the former precinct, especially when viewed from the riverside gardens, now accessible to the public. The possibility of restoring the moat system here is under consideration. A *potager* has been created beside the lake, practical as well as pedagogic in purpose.

Restoration of the eastern end of the church and cleaning of the chapter-house remains outside have recreated a hint of monastic ritual practice and made sense of some undistinguished heaps of building stone, the skeletons of former functional rooms. Gone are the unkempt appearance and faded ruins of romantic neglect, studded with plant growth, greened by an excess of moisture. It reminds us that the abbey was once new, a symbol of endeavour by a few dozen committed individuals united in spiritual community. The cleanliness that is said to go hand in hand with godliness now signals a more alert aura, a new half-life of didacticism and admiration. Cultural significance has replaced religious distinction, duty and responsibility have passed from the church to secular masters.

The rise and fall of silence has undulated through the valley over the centuries, contributing to its subtly persistent personality. Today summer visitors and events – particularly the choral concerts for which the abbey is well-known – emit little waves of sound into the habitual deep pool of quiet, but this is a place that suffers in its soul from cacophonous noise, like the trail bikes sometimes heard in the woods, and heavy footfall. Stillness, endurance, calm and order characterize a sense of co-operation in this place where man and nature have proved compatible.

The ancestral spirit of Le Relec can still be experienced today, most powerfully on August 15th, day of the annual Pardon. This event has changed over the years since I first attended, when a *fest deiz* followed the afternoon mass, but it was always a movingly authentic celebration of local people expressing their loyalty and identity in that most Breton of ways: through song and dance. Recently I joined a small procession carrying banners and the statue of Notre-Dame du Relec before mass began in mid-morning. There were only a couple of on-lookers among the many participants, who sang in honour of Our Lady as they marched, and of her chapel here like a welcoming nest, drawing the unhappy to a little place of shelter and succour. The simplicity of the sentiment enhanced its potency. Tears sprang to my eyes, not from any religious affiliation, but for tradition respected and sincerely practised, and the great emotional well that connects even the distant past and present. It is a day when the site seems to echo once more the undiluted values and beliefs of its founders.

Once the service was underway, I crossed the river and walked in the woods above the old waterside gardens of the monastery. From the church, the sound of Breton voices singing the Gloria in their ancient language swelled across the valley. No monk ever did greater honour to Le Relec than these modern faithful, adding their portion to the sound of centuries which has lingered in the highest spaces of the church in a canopy of continuous expression. There is an excellent acoustic here, and a special annual festival, Arrée Voce, celebrating choral music from around the world. In the 1980s an ambitious project was mooted to build a centre dedicated to this genre and the Breton tradition here. Imagine what changes to this quiet valley such a scheme might have brought, for good or ill.

After the closure of the abbey at the time of the Revolution, it was used as stabling, then sold in 1794 to a Morlaix merchant who intended to restore both church and cult. Later renovations and additions like the heraldic windows have little altered the uncomplicated impression within the church. Without monks in residence it is impossible to make sense of what a working abbey would have been like, but that the Cistercians laid the beginnings of a lasting project, an idea of responsible engagement is evident all around. The lasting remains or 'relics' in this valley are the signs of faith's practical application to landscape, a legacy of commitment to the land. The reassuring concurrence of natural beauty and functionality sums up the un-lost undercurrent of simple spirituality.

RUINS

Ruins are the shadow-selves of structures. Lost and abandoned, their lack of function and working purpose has separated them from human association and brought them into closer relationship with nature. The dirt of time clings to walls reclaimed by vegetation, which thrives on ruins, drawing nourishment from decay, settling into possession. Relics of man claimed by a greater power. The gentle conversation between stone and plants animates these lonely sites. Many a building is kept up by foliage, bound to the earth by stronger roots than construction can supply.

The causes of ruination are many. Neglect, deliberate destruction, vandalism, lack of money, abandonment are all possible factors. What's left on the site of a historical building is likely to be the bits too difficult to demount, cart away or recycle, perhaps why so many vaulted arches have remained. Apart from their material value as quarries for local construction projects, ruins offer a potent symbolism of temporal decay and the transience of human achievement. They have long served as artists' models for the picturesque, the romantic spirit and an idealization of the past. Decrepit castle walls shorn asunder speak of heroism rather than the brutality and violence of war, graceful tracery of an empty church window conjure up the pure simplicity of faith, not venal corruption and power games. We make things better than they are.

But why are we as individuals so drawn to ruins? A field of ruins can bring great structures down to our level, reducing status to an apologetic remnant. They make us happy and sad at the same time, a gratifying combination, with one eye on the exquisite melding of that most Breton green and grey in the landscape and the other on debilitation. They offer scope for our imagination and allow each individual to fill the empty spaces with his own ideals and nostalgias. There is more active participation in this experience than viewing a complete operative building, which tells rather than poses questions. And with the more stimulating challenge of ruins, we can supply any answers we like.

Abiding love for ruins is more than merely enjoyment of a romantic evocation of the past, or the pathetic image of faded glory. There is a special veneration reserved for survivors. Far from representing *memento mori*, ruins show us continuation after the end, the survival of essence. Looking objectively at ruins enables us to see ourselves in a linear context beyond a simply spatial one. The idea of endurance alongside decay appeals to our own sense of longevity and reinforces encouraging notions of resilience. I don't think about the end of our civilization – for want of a better word – when I linger among ruins.

There is a special authenticity about ruins, an air of Aeschylean suffering into truth. The impact of a strong visual identity affects us, whilst their shadows and missing parts hint at a lost complexity of character. We can feel in our bones the basic human affinity of being inside a place where life has been lived, but no longer, a general recognition of those well outside our own time-frame without the fine lines of period detail. It's the vicarious re-experiencing of experience. There is an ease in handling the memory of past in a safe way.

Certainly we can indulge in the poignant contrast between what was and what is, and the melancholy of impermanence. The sadness for this lost past is strangely comforting, a mix of idealised sentiment and realism. We can understand the cyclical nature of history as we see it in nature all the time. There is consolation in this patterning for that which must be lost. We also like history tinged with heartache, failure that is not all our own. We can identify with fragmentation, the reflection of our own lives and the lingering memories of glories that came to an end. Ruins present a 3D metaphor of everyman's triumphs and disasters, with the constant potential – or threat – of reconstruction.

What is the reality of ruins? Does it lie in the present or the past? When ruins are stripped of plants and cleansed of their acquired patina, the results can be disconcerting. The change of colour alone leads to a change of personality. A gleaming ruin is a strange half-life stage, reminding the structure of its original newness, whilst bringing it no nearer to completion of form or restoration of purpose. Remnants are given a helping hand in the name of preservation and educational heritage, whilst in all conscience they can never attain their original integrity. Poor old ruins, now required to perform, and with the natural process of decline arrested, doomed to an awkward perpetuation.

LOSTMARC'H

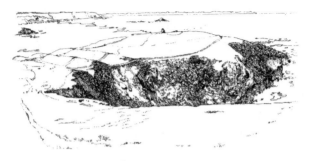

Extremity. One early morning a decade ago, I was walking on the Crozon peninsula, heading south from Castel Dinan on a beautiful summer day, along the undulating coastal path of this portentous shoreline. Passing over yet another headland through the stones of a natural barrier, suddenly I saw the dramatic fortified peninsula of Lostmarc'h below, starkly outlined in the clear air, waves pounding at the foot of its cliffs. This little promontory with its sharp bank and ditch defences pokes out into the Atlantic, more like a small green charm on the bracelet of dazzling coast that wends down to the Cap de la Chèvre than the horse's tail depicted in its name.

The sense of majesty with which we imbue such spectacular coastal scenery with all its potent combination of sea and stone is not limited to modern judgments of natural beauty. It must have been a factor in the siting of the major megalithic complex that once stood on the heath-covered hillside above the peninsula. There was a large *dolmen*, and still a few stunted *menhirs* can be seen, the single major survivor, impressive at 3m high, a beacon on the gorsy plateau. Their presence is indicative of a large alignment and ritual place, destroyed for building material in later ages. The Celts left these stones alone. In the Iron Age, the practicalities of defence for a community under threat were what mattered, using a natural feature of the landscape nearby as a basic site for improvement by man's hand.

Defence here was not of the highest point – the promontory of Lostmarc'h is actually quite low - but of the best protected, a fist of land sealed by steep cliffs on the seaward sides and a narrow isthmus joining it to the shore. At high tide the peninsula is cut off on three sides, belonging neither to ocean nor landmass. At the land-end of this *éperon barré* two lines of manmade high banks and deep ditches running across the neck mark the fortifications dating from the Iron Age, creating a tiny separate world sticking out into the sea, suspended from quiet routine, governed by rules of protection and preservation. It was the last refuge against attack, with an enclosed area large enough to house a few dozen men, women, children and animals in temporary shelters.

The extreme conditions at this edge point were unsuited to a properly developed residential village, and resources to support a community long-term did not lie close to hand. There were certainly iron deposits in the vicinity, but not enough to demand defence on a permanent basis. As Lostmarc'h is on the way to nowhere and far from meaningful centres of power and wealth, it was surely created in the face of local disputes long before the arrival of a muscular Roman army merited a defensible retreat. An enemy with any kind of patience or organized supply chain could hardly fail to triumph. It must have been a place of rapid attack and repulse or submission with associated slaughter. Beware of your neighbours.

Lostmarc'h is an edge place, where the thin line between security and insecurity is fragile, where vulnerability is borne on the wind and danger could come from land or sea. If the original use of this site for megalith installations was designed to draw attention to an important place of ritual ceremonies, by the Iron Age the peninsula was adapted to defend against such outside attentions. With the development of society, there was more to lose. Today our ingrained admiration of raw natural beauty (as it becomes rarer) obscures an appreciation of the sense of fear and threatening reality that often prevailed in 500BC. It was a time for readiness, a swift response to danger and risk.

This danger whether from incomers, raiders or speculators was sparked by the sight of sails or the warning word passed from village to village that hostility was on the move. The environment of Lostmarc'h turns accepted notions of peril on their head: high cliffs, high tides and high winds become measures of safety. The camp represents a suspension of normality. Families sheltering behind the defensive ditches and palisaded banks had nowhere to go, no further retreat from daily life. They looked to the elements for protection. It was about survival: posting guards, listening intently through the mist for sounds of threat, collecting water carried on the West wind from crevices in the rocks, penning the animals away from the precipitous edges. When the attack came and men leapt to arms, did women huddle in frightened silence with their children or grab weapons too and hurl abusive defiance at their foes?

Entering the camp through the once gated central gap shows quite a rise ahead, up to the small central plateau. It feels surprisingly small here. Although so open to the stupendous reach of sea and sky, there is still a sense of being confined and trapped, herded in like animals: in such a space there were no choices, except jumping from cliffs. At the far end the land falls again and below the final brink, nature and erosion have added a pincer defence in three dark curving claws of rock. Surrounded by the ambivalent sea, physical survival was precarious, the solid ground contained within crumbling cliffs, with their pillow lavas from quite another age pounded repeatedly by the waves.

When sight is not obscured by clammy mist, views from the promontory span the Tas de Pois and Pointe de Dinan to the north, the vast beaches of La Palue beyond that of Lostmarc'h with the war defences of a more modern age still on the sand, all the way down to the Cap de la Chèvre, and beyond across the sea to the Pointe du Van marking Cap Sizun. And yet even among so many edges, on Lostmarc'h one is super-conscious of edginess, a creeping sense that there is no way out. The scream of the wind is ominous. A foreboding impression of unattachment abides in this place without options but to fight or perish, the very last sight for the losers encompassing an elemental exuberance of sea and sky, narrowing the gap between seeing and being.

Lostmarc'h serves as a reminder of what can be defended against men in an age before gun-powder. It remains a symbol of the precarity of edge living, the particular context where edge is not a two way street, but THE END.

ST GUÉNOLÉ

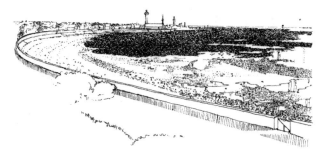

Exposure. This strange flat coast on the south-west tip of Finistère is a notorious danger-spot, not only for sailors on the sea. There is land where it shouldn't be, a coastal strip reclaimed from the marshes that still dominate the interior, lines of modern white houses, encrusted by the salt spray from which there is no escape. On the coastal walkway a common sight is figures struggling against the jarring wind, leaning far forwards to maintain their balance. Nothing separates man and the elements here in St Guénolé, one of the ports of Penmarc'h (named for its horse's head shape), together with Kerity and tiny St Pierre where the little chapel's fire tower once served as a warning to shipping before the advent of lighthouses.

The 15th century Chapelle de Notre-Dame de la Joie stands bravely right on the sea wall, an unbowed bastion against the worst of weathers, presenting its solid west face to all the sea can throw at it. The building has survived the most ferocious storms, filled in 1896 with pebbles and seaweed hurled by flood-water, but still intact. The figures on the *calvaire* are blurred by a blue-grey coating of sea moss, a legacy of such traumas. Ships carved outside and hung inside as votive offerings in the boat-shaped nave express gratitude for survival from shipwreck and Our Lady's patronage. By contrast with conventional piety, high up in the nave, the sculpted figure of an enticing siren combs her beautiful hair, and clutches a mirror to her bare breast. She, like the model ships, is a symbol of charm against the crack of timber, the chute into the dark water. Safety and preservation is worth any prayer to any potential source of help. Who knows the ocean better than a mermaid?

A great shelf of flat rock spreads a black stain out from the shore like a scalloped neckline, stark and innocuous at low tide, submerged and deadly when the water rises. Even in the 14th century the scenery was notorious, leaving a mark in European literature with Chaucer's *blakkes rokkes of Amorik that is called Britayne,* a key device of the plot in the Franklin's Tale, my set text for English A level at school. His heroine Dorigen paces the coast close to her castle home near Penmarc'h, watching the shipping pass out at sea and fearing for her beloved husband. Arveragus is in

England for jousting tournaments and she is convinced that on his return he will lose his life as the rocks menaced every vessel that drew close to the shore. She strikes a bargain with a magician who claims he can make the rocks disappear, although the terms of the deal threaten to break up her marriage once her husband is safely returned. Those deadly rocks remained in my imagination for all the time between then and now, when they are not only familiar in reality but part of my emotional landscape.

The rocks of St Guénolé have long been a threat not only to love, but life itself. Apart from the perilous shelf in the bay, huge striated outcrops north of the port, known simply as Les Rochers, are notorious for fatal accidents. They are too tempting a perch, and almost every year someone is taken by surprise and lost to a greedy wave. The archaeologist and artist Paul du Chatellier, whose little studio used to stand nearby, witnessed a terrible event in 1870. The family of the Prefect of Finistère, enjoying a picnic on a fine day on these rocks, were swept away. Only three of the five bodies were ever recovered. An iron cross set into the stone now marks the inauspicious spot.

The element of danger in the midst of everyday life lies at the heart of the character of this place. Normality is often extreme. Exceptional spring tides on the prostrate shore draw many for the spectacle of thunderous watery mountains looming over the low land and the curious phenomenon of thick white sea foam filling creeks and inlets like heavy snow drifts and enveloping the harbour buildings in a coat of cotton-wool. In stormy weather all definition is lost as the huge sky and huge sea merge into a boiling mass of grey and black threaded by flashes of silver. The machinations of air drive all before it, smashing onto a coast unprotectable against such onslaughts. Water rises and falls, breaths are held and released as the aching clamour of the tempest drops, throbbing in the ears subsides and the familiar smell of briny spoil replaces that of fear.

The eerie formation of the flat rocks is the result of tectonic plate movement billions of years ago. To walk out there at safe low tide is to enter a strange horizontal world between worlds, here slabbed like a causeway towards Île Nonna, there in small wrinkled blocks like a series of miniature grey towns constructed around lakes of submerged seaweed and encircled by maroon and green hills as Irish moss, dulse, sea-lettuce and red spaghetti drape the rocks, and mini-deserts made of sand are rendered crunchy by a million tiny shells. Gulls strut, terns and turnstones do their business, whilst crabs hide. There's something hypnotic about this mass and its sulphurous scent, so solid and still *en masse*, but at close sight enlivened by a myriad of quick movements.

Beyond by contrast are the striking verticals of the chapel spire, the earliest lighthouse and the magnificent towering Phare Eckmühl (1897) looming like megaliths over this prone kingdom. The latter is handsomely constructed of Kersanton stone, 66m high, with an octagonal tower and sophisticated design detail, with a frieze of stylised waves decorating the base. It is an alluring beacon, mesmerizing at night as the black water merges with the black rocks and the tremendous flare rakes land and sea with its message of hope.

Survival and salvation, twin secret thrills twisted out of grief, loss and loneliness in the far corner of Finistère.

CHAPELLE SAINT SAMSON

Eternity. Near the stone citadel of the rocks of Landunvez stands the tiny chapel of St Samson, announced from the land-side by its simple stone cross. Below on the shore edge is a *fontaine* and another wonky cross looking out to sea. Face the ocean, turn away from the modern houses across the coast road and this place feels remote. Beyond an off-shore rocky fringe that was once land itself there is nothing directly westward. No island, no landfall. Nothing before what was once called the New World more than five thousand kilometres away. Only an enormity of water.

Unseen further north is that part of the old world from which the Breton saints emerged. St Samson, from the abbey of Llanwit Major in Wales, is perhaps the greatest of them all, if only because he actually existed, unlike many of his more nebulous colleagues. He became bishop of Dol-de-Bretagne, held in esteem by the Emperor of the Franks and present at important gatherings of the Roman church. His name is on a document from the Council of Paris c.555, ten years before his death.

Samson did not arrive from Great Britain in this lonely spot, but elsewhere, in the far east of Brittany. No-one in their right minds would have tried to land here. Boulders litter the tiny inlet, a giant's quarry where any errant little craft would have been dashed to smithereens in an instant on this unforgiving shore. The chapel does not commemorate a heroic landing, and the connection with Samson is vague, un-illuminated by any personal association with the saint or miracle-working such as he performed near Dol. The surviving chapel dates from 1785, replacing an earlier medieval structure. The *fontaine* was said to cure eye problems and help children slow to walk, a focal point of potential healing for believers.

This site is a physical expression of the relationship of place and faith, but it has a long pre-Christian pedigree, once marked by a *menhir*, a standing-stone 2m high, which suggests the possible motive for Christianization, an assertion of the new religion on the site of the old. Local tradition says that rubbing against the *menhir* was a cure for rheumatism, but why was the stone placed here originally? There is no shortage of spectacular coastline in north-west Finistere, yet this spot is special. Perhaps the sacred association is simply water.

This is surely a place to celebrate such an elementary miracle, but water as the basic life-giving force, not the fancy stuff of healing. Not water tamed and framed by a stone wall built by man, but the crux of survival. Giving humble thanks for a simple source is a positive kind of religious fundamentalism. Before one can be grateful for any quality of life, life itself has to be sustained, and water is the essential.

One spring on this site is capped by the *fontaine* and led from there by a stone channel to filter down towards the sea, greening as it goes. The other is close by, passing under the coast path, dribbling past clumps of yellow fleabane in a reedy line, aiming for the salt water below. Sweet sources representing the basis of existence trickle down the low cliff to merge with ocean. They deserve the focus of honour in this place, balancing in their invigorating gift the destructive power of ocean which will ultimately prevail over a disintegrating coastline.

The low coast here is topped by infertile *landes*, maritime heath of coarse grass and plants whose roots bind the sandy soil. Wind and water dominate the scene, the south-west breeze bringing in the scent of the wider sea like an unwrapped present for shore-dwellers. It links here to the faraway and opens pathways to the unknown; just as establishing ritual in a place like this reaches out to infinity.

Here faith and hope of one sort or another have a long history: an original impulse of connection in the Neolithic with the placing of at least one standing-stone, a Bronze Age stone, a chapel, renewed over time and the crosses: X marks the spot of faith. There's connection with the boundlessness inherent in belief. It is not the epitome of 'peace and tranquillity' strangely claimed in tourist-speak and belied by the crash of incoming waves, but a place that stirs the spirit and our subconscious seas.

The limitless quality of ocean reflects the relationship between place and faith, the shortness of the step between land and sea, now and eternity. The barrier of rocky armour hugging the shore is a frontier point between life and a last journey, big issues in a small setting, and the clinging humility of faith the most honest response in this most patulous of places.

SACRED GEOGRAPHY

Land itself was once sacred when inherently bound up with rural communities dependent on its bounty. The lack of human control over nature was apparent in floods and storms, failed harvest and deathly cold. Before rational thought, organized religion and scientific investigation separated us from nature, what was and what could be came at the will of gods or spirits which must be propitiated and appeased.

The earliest constructors in the Neolithic period began to mark the landscape with burial chambers, standing-stones and cairns, and to practise 'religious' ritual at these sites. Their concerns seem to have been with the passage between life and death, and the continuity inherent in honouring the ancestors. It is difficult to speak of deities with any certainty, although the cosmological alignment of certain sites and the womb-like underground spaces may connect with a sky god above and a fertility goddess, or Mother Earth herself. Some *menhirs* may well have been indicators of boundaries and territorial rights, nominally ratified by the will of superior powers which were feted in the ceremonies whose faint traces have been brought back to us by painstaking archaeological research.

Until relatively recent times, the megaliths were thought to be the work of either giants or the Iron Age civilization of the Armorican peninsula. It isn't just poor chronology and unscientific analysis that makes the anachronistic Celtic connection so common. The animals and birds once carved on *menhirs* suggest a semi-animism that fits the much later Celtic cosmology, when the whole landscape was enlivened by a million spirits of growth, when rivers and springs were worshipped for their life-giving properties and the oak tree took on the symbolism of Druidic lore. An awareness of and reverence for the life force manifested in nature, and a respect for patterns of being other than those of humankind lay at the heart of Celtic religion, a trait exposed repeatedly in song and poetic perception of the environment.

The close connection of Celtic religion and natural forces expressed in seasonal and open-air ritual made the landscape a target for the missionary zeal of early Christianity. In Brittany the laying down of sacred geography becomes emphatic with the arrival of saints from Great Britain, missionaries bringing the word of the Christian god to the undeveloped west, not yet touched by the firm hand of the Church of Rome like towns further east. They were to interpose a new layer of hierarchy where God the creator was above nature and the sole arbiter of man's destiny.

Early hagiographies are full of geographical reference. The setting and the landscape are important factors of the story being created. Saints repeatedly exerted their powers – lent by God – over wild paganism, the people and places they found on arrival. The rooting out of brambles and eviction of savage creatures living in that untamed vegetation were part of an essential phase of establishing Christianity. It was a literal and metaphorical sweep of the new broom. Land was cleared for the first settlements around primitive churches, forest areas razed to the ground, seeds planted, new crops harvested, all in the name of the incoming religion. It was said that St Ronan took over a Celtic *nemeton* or sacred space as his own ritual context in the landscape and that he walked the boundaries of this territory each day.

The close bond between peasants and their land which led to belief in plant and animal spirits, as well as the animism of stones, trees and streams, now had to be sanctioned through the intervention of Christianity. Personal ties were redirected and retied, binding the people to the church and the powers of its ministers, relating the real life of ordinary people to mystical process of religious faith through the medium of human constructs rather than natural wonder and the original sense of awe in the landscape. The miracle of the Resurrection replaced pragmatic aspects of earlier religion when a more reciprocal relationship with gods was envisaged, and sacrifice or offerings might lead in return to good weather and a bumper harvest.

When St Pol was given land by the local lord Withur, he first had to expel the wild inhabitants, including a bear, that lived there. He rid the Île de Batz of a marauding dragon, that ultimate symbol of rampant paganism, leading it by his bishop's stole like a dog on a lead, before forcing the great beast from the rocks into the sea at a spot still bearing the name Toul ar Serpent, Serpent's Hole. The huge Neolithic standing stone Men Marz (later Christianized by the addition of a puny cross) was said to have been placed on the coast by St Pol (or his sister) as a marker beyond which he forbade the sea to encroach, after flooding had badly affected people's lives. Here the saint puts himself - by virtue of the power of God invested in him - above nature, and sends the message of putting trust solely in the new divinity on the block: turn away from idolatrous megaliths and Celtic pluralism.

St Hervé and St Brieuc were both famed for their miraculous taming of wolves, which became docile and submissive under the power of the cross, but an anecdote from the life of the latter also describes the land-clearing undertaken for his new monastery. St Brieuc had many trees cut down in the forest to clear space and provide timber for construction. An early account of his life claims that local people were astonished at this swift transformation, another analogy of the suppression of wilderness by civilization, Christian power to transform landscape and shape nature to its will.

The reasons behind this strategy were many. Christianity offered man defence against the power of nature that had hitherto controlled and dominated people's lives. Christ was a man offering a way to conquer death, so often faced in difficult terrain. The miracles of the saints aped the powers of older deities, giving the Christian God victory in his rivalry with Nature. The lamb triumphed over the wolf and the dragon. Taking this control of the landscape drove a wedge between man and the animated landscape of the Celtic world. Lore was berated as superstition and the intimacy of the sacred bond with the earth was broken. Spontaneity of inter-action with the natural world was stifled, pushed aside by the performing priest whose presence was a reminder of God's constant interference in the fey world.

A new physical context was created in the early settlements around the church, places still there today, bearing the names of their founders – Plouneour, Lampaul, Lannédern – with prefixes indicating the first parishes (*plou*) and the holy places of saints (*loc*, *lan*). Social bonds came to be established around the nucleus of the church. This was the context in which people came to see and identify themselves, the small village, watched over by the ultimate landlord, God. Christianity was ever didactic, the saints with their book learning and intellectual knowledge were instructors for an illiterate population, spelling out the Christian message, the new rules and responsibilities of chosen souls, destined for life after death through the sacrifice of Christ. Resurrection was no longer the renewal of nature, but triumph in the name of the Lord. This could not help but influence the way in which people saw the land around them. It was to be exploited and made to work for a higher master, undermining the old sense of partnership and shared endeavour.

Triumphalism was a crucial part of early Christianity, the demonstration that the saints trumped pagan deities and disdained the Celtic Druid priesthood with their bloodthirsty rites and diabolical magic. It was a competition, and God enjoyed widespread initial victories. Over time, pagan sites were overridden. Crosses and chapels appeared near springs and rivers or on top of hills or standing-stones. It was a show of super-confidence: a statement of determined intent or a process of assimilation depending on your point of view. The movement of the Breton saints across the territory and later pilgrimage trails traced out sacred spots and focal points of Christian worship, imprinting their values and criteria on the local map. The landscape became a tool of the Church, a means to an end, controlled.

Landscape is all about layers, in its geological origins and development, its subterranean and surface exploitation by men. Changing historical and cultural perceptions have imposed their own strata over the centuries, significantly at the time when early Christianity was setting its roots, introducing a new tier, based on the premise that God was more worthy of trust than fickle Nature, more reliable than the vagaries of weather which have given such beauty to western Brittany.

COAST

Coast is the unpicked hem of land's skirt, a fringe of
frayed nerves.

The littoral is an uncertain sort of place. Bits fall off.
Other bits move along. Spillage is of the essence.
People arrive. Some are aggressive; worse, some want
to convert you. Many leave of their own accord.
Coming and going. The waves arrive, blue or black
like bruises. Dangerous place, the coast. And all the
time, the amoral sea goes in and out, in and out with
no discrimination.

Between the sea of death and the land of life, coast is
a buffer zone, a threshold, a portal, a place of
mutation. The significant word is Between. The
shore cries out for propitiation which ever way you
are coming. Or going.
Which is more use on the coast,
psychopomp or life-guard?

The girl was seized by pirates. A stroll by the sea led
to onboard lechery. Ready to die rather than submit,
she flung herself into the water. But on the point of

drowning, a little fish carried her up, up, up to the shore. She ran home. And went on running, three times around the little house where her parents were playing gin rummy and not even thinking yet about supper, and then she fell down dead in front of the door.

Had she already crossed one threshold too many?

Things are brought in and out. Under surveillance: cargo, booty, fish and spies. Get in or get out before it is too late. Coast is limited time, purpose found or lost quickly. There are all kinds of wrecked hopes and filtered ingenuity left on the shore. How can you tell if the light shines out to save or squander life?

Less working more watching now, fixed on the hypnotic murderousness of the cobra sea. The boy from the coast, disappointed at first sight of a tree, grows old still keeping his line of vision open. Edge people are watchful: waiting and wondering and getting the answer by absence. The coast is the place where things fail to appear.

Which way should you look first before crossing the shore?

ROSCOFF

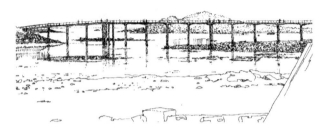

Perspective. The sea laps at the foot of the hotel. From the balcony of my room I look at the seascape. A sweeping view takes in the Chapelle Ste-Barbe faintly lit on its mound like a white ghost, wispy-edged, then the port area, still bright, with boats tucked safely in the curve of the harbour wall, and, across the water, the Île de Batz, a short orange strip emanating from another world. Looking down on the water offers a new perspective, the true slant of currents, wintry moon-light shimmering on every tiny cadence like a million birds with wings spread in flight. Above the water-line in a swiftly darkening foreground is a bridge apparently to nowhere.

Roscoff is an old town, a maritime chameleon. It is the familiar of commerce, piracy, fishing, war-time subterfuge, seaweed and thalassotherapy. Miniature stone cannons on the church tower point towards the old enemy England, via an open and surreptitious route of exchange that has served both sides of the Channel well. Vikings, corsairs, pirates, merchants, smugglers, chancers, spies and secret agents have profited from this stretch of sea and its snaggy coastline in war and peace, the frisson of precarious times adding to the satisfaction of transaction in getting the better of someone.

Water gives this variety of experience. It attracts us more than all other elements because we can see, hear, touch, taste and smell it with ease. We are so much water ourselves, it takes little to infiltrate our being. As night falls early over the town, the moon drives along a silver road over the sea, between sombre crocodiles of rock that menace more in the dark than daylight. Nautical lights blaze - red, green, silver - each regular in its own sequence but the combination produces a screen of mad frenetic flashing, keeping alive the notion of danger against an ominous calm before the tide turns. *Wwa, wwa, wwa* comes the yell of a gull, crisp in the December night air. *Huwhee* comes sharply from the secrecy of black rock. The compulsive beeping of the sandpipers has fallen silent at last. The slim arc of the footbridge ends in a nothingness of inky water.

After a clear night, morning and low tide bring streaks of yellow and grey to the foreshore, the sea beyond a light aquamarine. The footbridge, constructed in

1967-9 to enable the regular ferry to the Île de Batz to operate at low tide, strides starkly across the sand on its 50 plus concrete pillars. Predators stalk the exposed beach, while a resting egret shakes itself into a great puffy feathery white ball. My balcony is on a level with the shrieking herring gulls, and one lands imperiously on the rail inches away, giving me the yellow eye of acquisitive threat. The air smells of wet wood, bladderwrack and brine, with a light tang of engine-oil brought in bursts on the breeze. The constancy of coastal rhythms throbs gently in a renewal of purposeful activity around the port.

Already there is also movement on the footbridge. A man and his dog walk steadily out along this narrow pier. The actual footfall in no way reflects the original intermittent function of ferry access. All through the day men, women, children and pets make the 590m long trek and at the end, simply turn back to retrace their steps. This is a fine small-scale example of the importance of journey not destination. The return offers a new perspective on the town, an outsider's sense of arrival, but in a spirit of slow appreciation that freedom of movement allows, unlike so many before in more clandestine moments.

It is there, so must be walked. No-one can resist a path. There's no such place as nowhere.

OUESSANT

Otherness. Ouessant (Breton Enez Eusa, English Ushant) is a long 25 kilometres from the mainland. From Brest or Le Conquet a real journey is needed, with a stop at Molène en route, and then the sense of going beyond the beyond as that small island is left behind and the boat picks up speed seemingly into an uncharted wilderness, remote from the tame and civilised world. Jacques Cambry in his *Voyage dans le Finistère* (1794-5) refers to an oral tradition that Ouessant was actually the fabled *ultima Thule* of classical authors. It doesn't quite fit with the geographer Pytheas' description of a semi-polar region six days sail from Britain, but the island exudes enough of a sense of separation to conjure up an image of the western edge of the known world.

The Passage du Fromveur separating Ouessant and the Molène archipelago is an ill-tempered stretch of complicated water named from the Breton *froud* (current) and *meur* (great) for the cross-purposes of its winds and currents, the latter turning about with the rise and fall of each tide. This five nautical mile zone was the scene of numerous shipwrecks until the creation of the supervised *rail de Ouessant* to the north of the island prevented large cargo vessels from taking a perilous short-cut and left the passage to fishing boats and ferries better manned to deal with its specificities on a daily basis.

The approach to port presents an immediate impression of wildness: stark cliffs rise up and there is no welcoming snug harbour with a comforting line of houses and a bar or two. The port is like an afterthought, an intrusion in the face of the rude nature that dominates this island. In times of severe weather the ferry has to use the port of the bourg of Lampaul, the only commercial centre, four kilometres away at the opposite end of the island.

The paradox of Ouessant is that for all this lonely imagery of isolation, the island is in some senses the most international of locations. Excavations over twenty years at Mez Notariou have revealed a Bronze Age settlement from c.1500BC and an Iron Age village almost adjacent. Finds on the site from all over Europe attest Ouessant's important position for travellers moving between south and north, commanding as it does the tricky entry to the Channel. The pottery paralleled in style with a site in Switzerland puts the island on the contemporary cultural map of the continent.

In fact Ouessant is not remote, but a place of passage. A more sobering indication of its globally diverse connections is the proliferation of wreckage encircling the island: an American ship carrying cocoa, rice and tobacco in 1739, an English brig full of salt in 1817, an Austrian ship taking coal from Swansea to Trieste in 1908, the Russian Vostok in 1978 with that most useful of cargoes for a treeless island – planks. These are but a few in a long list of vessels that failed to negotiate the tumultuous waters surrounding this hard land.

The island itself has a history of austerity for man and a richness of nature surprising in such a weather-swept landscape. At 8 x 3.5 km and 1550 hectares it is a sizeable place, split along an east-west fault-line, now a lush green valley of low trees, reservoirs and sources of fresh-water topped by stone *lavoirs* in the scattered hamlets. Traditionally the houses are white-washed with blue shutters, the archetypal colours of the island. No garish constructions by wealthy incomers spoil the profound simplicity. In the bourg of Lampaul there are flowers everywhere, pink and white valerian exploding like fireworks from the high stone walls, every garden planted to burst out in technicolour as early as the seasons allow.

On the swaths of pasture and cliff-top *landes*, a coloured hodgepodge of wild flowers has replaced the traditional patchwork of tiny walled plots of land which once covered the island, the women's domain of production, as men laboured far away in the service of the French navy. Star-shaped sheep shelters remain here and there, designed to offer relief from the multi-directional blasts of wind. On the springy surface of the moors, are gorse – in places deliberately cultivated within walls for fuel and fodder – heather and bright flowers of fresh broom which pop up while the wind tells their flattened foliage to stay low. Thrift, scabious, wild thyme and honey-suckle vivify the grassy plains.

The sea has always beaten the imaginative, putative and everyday rhythm of this place. Local legends feature the Morganed and Morganezed, merpeople who live in the ocean and sport on the shore, enjoying unpredictable contact with humans. Reality is about life at the behest of the elements. Ouessant itself is the strong, solid hub at the centre of turbulence, ringed by lighthouses protective of mariners and islanders alike. On the north-eastern and highest point is Le Stiff, the oldest still working example in France, ordered by Vauban in

1695 and now looking like a functional furuncle beside the elegant grace of the 75m radar tower built in 1982.

The ragged edge of the north coast from Le Stiff to the Pointe de Pern has borne the brunt of the weather and tides, raw rock faces like eviscerated innards of the earth, the granite slowly disintegrating via fissures where the insidious moisture of the salt air has penetrated. Fantastic formations contribute to the sense of rough brute creation, a work hewn of gigantic movements over aeons of time, a work in progress if the elements have their savage way, shearing off any tell-tale friability. Looking seaward beyond the Île de Keller with the eerie outline of its single house, there is only ocean, often merging into a misty, muzzy soft blue-grey of sky.

Past the Bay of Calgrac'h, the iconic black and white striped Phare de Creac'h (1863) dominates the view. This contains the museum of Phares et Balises, presenting the evolving techniques of maritime communication and the great work of lighthouse construction in hazardous conditions, a summary of man's response to the challenges of sky and sea. This is an environment that thrusts man so indelibly into often dangerous relationship with the natural world and the self, the struggle between introspection and social connection.

The Pointe de Pern at the western extremity of the island defines the turbulence and relentless savagery of the sea that is the body to Ouessant's heart. The lighthouse of Le Nividic and its two redundant pylons rise above the treacherous knobs of rock and ruthless whirling breakers. The seethe of currents pushes and shoves in all directions, constantly sparring like an unruly mob bent on violence. When mist obscured the early lantern's beam, only the echo of a fog-horn could give a warning beyond the narrow visibility. The ruined building on the point once housed this simple device, based on a compressed air tank and powered by horses at its inauguration in 1866. Steam was soon preferred as the free-ranging animals had proved unresponsive to urgency.

The southern shores of the island offer a softer profile, facing Molène and its cluster of islets across the Fromveur. Here mica-schist predominates, headlands punctuated by the only real beaches, but the water is always on the chilly side. High on Penn Arlan stands a Neolithic stone circle near the solitary cliff-top Croix de St-Pol, dating from 1704, with the saint's stone boat nearby, bearing the indentations of his praying knees. He is said to have arrived from Britain near this spot and chased away the pagan priestesses who then moved as far from him as possible to the other end of the island where there was later said to be a large pagan temple at the Pointe de Pern. The vibrancy of paganism in this remote place far from the rules and restrictions of church and civil powers may have been the original impetus for St Pol's mission.

Ouessant's outstanding personality stems from this sense of separation, an otherness that operates by its own rules, too far from censure to care for the eyes of any world beyond those heaving waters. Indigenous customs reflected a unique way of living. The *proella*, attested at least from the 18th century, was a special funerary rite for those whose remains were never recovered, tossed forever in near or far off seas. A tiny wax cross stood as substitute for the dead. The priest performed the funeral service in the church, before placing the cross in a wooden urn, attached to a pillar in the nave and decorated with a sculpted cloth marked by tears like tadpoles. There it would wait, perhaps not alone, for the visit of a bishop or missionary to the island to be ceremonially placed in a small mausoleum in the cemetery designed for this purpose. This is conspicuous by the unique north-south alignment, making the small structure stand out from the traditionally appointed crowd of graves.

The island, as indescribable as unforgettable, holds on to its own.

PONT KRAC'H

Transition. A bridge is a connective principle between two separate points, a crossing place from one side to another. It's a stage on a linear journey, but Pont Krac'h adds another spatial dimension: as the tide rises, it disappears. Now you see it, now you don't. A part-time bridge, not fully fit for purpose. Hours pass and the immense causeway emerges again, draped with seaweed like an elaborate table-setting festooning the massed granite slabs. This twice-daily striptease act, a dressing and undressing of stone, is a mesmerizing feat of revelation. The place has haunted my imagination for many years. The first time I saw it, the bridge wasn't there.

The wide valley of the Aber Wrac'h between Plouguerneau and Lannilis is closely wooded, the land rising higher on the north side. When the tide is up, it is an impressively broad expanse of grey water, lapping at the low trees on either side, concealing the bridge below. The positioning of the structure was dictated by a tapered point between two wide creeks. At low tide a veritable desert of undulating sand and mud banks reveal the mere tiny channel of ever-flowing river that passes under the central arch of the bridge. But this place is all about process and transformation. Watching the long, slow out-breath of the tidal estuary blow upstream and then draw back is to be involved in an active meditation on flow.

Hours after the tide begins to retreat to its true love ocean, the water suddenly offers a shimmering simulacrum, a creation of light on the surface, where a deceptive breeze continues to push upstream even as the undertow pulls back out. I watch from a rocky point well above the non-existent bridge in unaccountably tense anticipation as the sense and shape of it appear long before the stones themselves are revealed. Lines form on the water. This ghostly eddying echo frizzles the surface, a liquid outline of what lies below, a nuance of bridge. The ends come free first, sticky dark boulders and the stunted stone cross, but what links the two sides is obscure. Then slowly, slowly, slowly comes the revelation: water's slick motion is broken up into a marvellous pattern as it gradually gives up temporary power over the bridge's existence, reluctantly sliding off the stones, leaving a glistening mass of dark seaweed and crinkly autumn leaves edging the grey causeway. From my vantage point, it's like a huge scaly monster rearing up from the water, as if the bridge is rising rather than the water falling. Indeed the structure's persona is more animal than mineral.

Pont Krac'h is elusive in other ways. It may be the work of Iron Age Cyclopean hands, with its great granite blocks – a millstone from this period was found in the vicinity - or even as much as 1500 years later. Was it an expression of the collective man-power of an expansive Celtic tribe, or a structure contemporary with the earliest castle-building, constructed at the behest of a local lord? Archaeologists do not agree. Nor is there any consensus about the name. On a map of 1630 it appears as Pont Grac'h, maybe signifying an old woman, a witch or a fish, the same connotations as the Aber Wrac'h itself. In French today it is labelled Pont du Diable, Devil's Bridge. Work of renovation to stabilize the remains of the great structure took place in 2007-8, after a huge clearance of clinging seaweed, re-defining the arches that allow the flow of water. The Devil himself turned up to celebrate a new inauguration. What was once important as a place of passage is now to derive its identity from notional historical merit.

The bridge was bought by a local land-owner in 1789, and he oversaw the construction of a mill on the

Plouguerneau side. Other millers upstream claimed this obstructed their livelihood, and in the early 19th century, some even argued for the destruction of the bridge, claiming it was too dangerous to cross, a great useless heap of stones. There was no sense of historic value then, in an age driven solely by economic constraints, although when improvements and a passage for boats were suggested in 1823, both communes refused the opportunity for development. In the 1850s a bridge replaced the ferry downstream where the current Pont de Paluden (1933) stands.

Of course there is a legend. How could such an extraordinary feat of early engineering escape the attentions of the church and local superstition. The Devil, whose affinity with stone and aptitude as a constructor of remarkable speed are well-known, was the original architect. He struck a bargain with the miller, who was fed up with trailing his wares by cart up to the head of the estuary, to build a bridge across the river in a single night (for the Devil is a fast worker) in exchange for the first soul to cross. It was one of those deals made late at night after drink's been taken without too much thought for the small print.

In the morning, the Devil had kept his part of the bargain. No more would the miller have to labour along all those extra miles. He stepped onto the new bridge with a bulging flour sack over his shoulder and made his way ponderously to the middle. There he let his cat out of the bag and the Devil had to content himself with a feline soul. He has had his revenge, they say, with many a drunken traveller failing to make the crossing safely over the years. It was not such a bad deal for the Red Man after all: a whole bunch of sodden souls. And still his work stands, exciting admiration and respect.

How something as practical as a bridge can acquire an atmosphere of magic and mystery is by virtue of change of circumstance and changing attitudes to the past. Both the building of an alternative road bridge and the rise of water levels over the last 2000 years have contributed to the lonely episodic persona of this bridge, felt even when unseen. A crossing once purposefully animated by people, horses and cattle has fallen into the quiet embrace of its wooded banks. It is now a destination in its own right, goal of fishermen, walkers and wonderers.

Any crossing point was a place of propitiation in the ancient world. Water was always dangerous. No-one was blasé about the power of tides and floods, and because swimming was not an everyday skill, drowning was a common form of death. The Celts made offering to the spirits or gods of rivers and marshy causeways wherever a way lay through any kingdom of water. A real rite of passage. Broken weapons, jewellery, any items of value might emerge many centuries later from the sludge. At Pont Krac'h a stone cross marks the southern entrance to the point of passage, doubtless a Christian echo of much earlier rites, a prayer for safety and survival amid the ebb and flow of the tide.

At low tide the mud banks are well-occupied with bird life, still egret and heron like a pair of bookends, gulls circling the thin strip of remaining water fringed upriver by ridges of exposed sand where a fisherman moves stealthily from spot to spot. The only sound is a low throb of water beneath the central arch at the bridge's sunken nipped-in waist. The causeway with its alluringly intricate slabs resembling the skin of a rusty grey snake offers an irresistible promise of connection, an invitation to cross despite the damp, algal slipperiness. I pick a careful way across the massive stones through a welcoming red carpet of seaweed, stepping onto and into at one and the same time.

Pont Krac'h is a place of ultimate fluidity. It is both under and over, a situation which is never finished or complete but ever in transition. Like those who crossed and still cross it today, the bridge is always coming and going, never here to stay.

WHAT'S IN A PLACE NAME?

With a name, space becomes a place

Geographical glue for man's environment

Knowing the name of a place is a badge of belonging

Knowing how to give directions is control over
strangers.

Territorial affection breeds protean vocabulary

From simple words of shape and structure

To the bounty of Earth defined a myriad ways

Names celebrate nature.

Then toponyms become self-referential: the founder,
the owner.

They record man's constructions.

They record the memory of human action.

They become the anchor of community.

Naming says power and possession, a claim on the land.

Place an ideological issue: taming the wilderness.

Saints and miracles construct social identity.

Names enhance and distort, privilege and pretend: heroes and devils

To attract a crowd.

Woeful that Arthur is a better draw than nature itself.

Rather a rock be Big or Broken or Beautiful or Brilliant, but belong to no-one.

A MATTER OF SCALE

More and more I become aware that the attractiveness of Brittany's landscape to a great many people is a matter of scale. There are no extremes here, neither of terrain nor temperature, and the degree of comfort and security that confers is a major factor in connectedness. It is often the difference between feeling oneself within a landscape rather than looking at it from the outside, which inevitably carries a degree of emotional detachment.

This is partly a matter of age - as we get older we start to seek peace from our surroundings, a reassurance relevant to our size and powers of endurance, rather than challenge or adventure or otherness. This is not a devaluation of experience, however, as our perception of significance is simply magnified in a smaller sphere.

Brittany's highest 'mountains', the Monts d'Arrée, reach up less than 400 metres, the most towering cliffs barely stand 100 metres above the sea. But these bald figures are quite irrelevant to impressiveness of the scenery, which is determined by context not comparison. These are magnificent settings in which to place ourselves.

So we can be 'on top of the world' on Mont-St-Michel-de-Brasparts or Menez Hom or 'at the end of the earth' at the Pointe de Corsen or the Pointe du Raz without becoming mountaineers or endurance hikers. And there we can feel our surroundings spectacular in a proportionate way to our own existence in the same world.

CHAOS DE MARDOUL

Reflection. The chaos of Mardoul is not remote, but it is a place apart. My *nemeton*, my sacred space. It's also my refuge. This short stretch of the Elez simulates an invisible enclosure bounded by walls of tree and stone, with a carpet of water, an atectonic shrine to the elements. Curious movement, the intrinsic dynamism of landscape, emanates from the valley in a harmony of sound and silence, motion and stillness.

Physically, the whole is contained between double bridges. At each end there is a low recent version up to bearing the weight of tractors passing to the nearby fields, but the manmade glory of the river landscape are the two old slab crossings for this ancient ford. One of these has a strong width of four stones, the other, flawed, is filled in with metal grid and rails. All are the evidence of passage and traffic, although the *ésprit de lieu* has miraculously survived the hand of man and the surrounding development of agriculture.

It starts and stops abruptly, this section of rocky chaos as the river Elez runs before and after without obstacle. Gone is the original shaping of the valley which caused a tumble of granite boulders into the river bed aeons ago. Now one side retains gentle height, a barrier of stone, both gigantic - a reminder of the original scale of the massif broken by wind and water - and unobtrusive, mingled with the flora of the moors, gorse, broom and bracken. The other side has been flattened by quarrying, a bubbling sea of humpy boulders reaching towards the isolated human habitation - an unobtrusive gîte - just visible through the trees. Here low ridges of rock protrude from the earth like horizontal steps across the path. The mark of tools is on the stones, grass growing from the wounds like balm; a sheered wedge set in the river itself bears witness to human exploitation.

In this enclave, the Elez descends in a series of shallow steps. All around the river, rocks, the spawn of earth, nestle in lying comfort on the banks, garnished with mosses in many forms, buoyantly green like miniature fields sprouting tufts from the granite bedrock, or patchy as a map. Some sport a slip-cover of lichen, others are so closely knit with their coating that moss and rock are one and inseparable to the eye, the hanger-on taking on the shades of its host, in a play of greys and silvers, the nuance of aging in glaucous shades.

The chaos is elongated, rocks fallen flatly, driven apart by the flow of water and smoothed down like a stone road, stepping-stones giving access to a still perch inside a vortex. Most are covered when the level rises to wintry heights, flooding the lower ground along the south bank. The movement of water is a complex pattern based on the unseen underneath, dark lines of submersion. Strands of sound as complex as a symphony are repeated and rephrased, themes both careless and insistent. On approach from the little access road, the notes seem separate and soothing, the string-quartet of babbling stream, but it mounts towards the climax of an orchestral movement in the clamour at the heart of the chaos.

Water's words to stone here are alternately loving and savage, caresses turn violent, stroking becomes a slap. In wild weather it is a seething insistence of water. All that rock can do is hold to itself, edges rounded to ease the onslaught and survive the longest time under a constant assault that is both smooth and brutal. It's an unequal contest in the end. The river can spread to mount its challenge: the rocks have no more movement in them. In dancing steps the water constantly changes direction, twisting, turning, preening round its static partner, forming shapes and ritual traces, like little tripping thoughts of happy times. As water tires of obstacle, there's the trumpet of torrent and torment, a surge of force. Under an angry wind, white-topped waves rage down the valley. In gentler times, with little explosions of foam like a series of sneezes, it glides as clear as glass down a shelf of rock. The old war between rock and water is a lost cause for the remnants of another earth. The river will have its way, hard or easy.

When calm, the channel is a mirror of shimmering reflections, water of absolute clarity like a canvas for trees and clouds, scenes pulled down from the sky to be framed between the rocks, yellow granite sand gleaming up from the riverbed behind the skeletal outlines of branches and reeds. Still or perturbed, reflection is an extra layer of perception, between the upper world and whatever lurks beneath those silhouettes of frail stalks and boughs. It offers a magical three dimensional reality, thought extended beyond the here and now into a deep meditative space.

Two round stone basins sit in the flow by the northern bank, broken-rimmed, like sunken crenellated towers,

123

green sludge in the bottom, a shiny surface circling the image of ragged winter trees, facing the demanding stream with the resignation of habit. These mysterious containers are prosaically claimed by history for the processing of flax, or more imaginatively postulated as Celtic ritual vessels, hostages of some river god that once deserved propitiation. It only needs anomaly, artifice within nature, to start a story. Here, where man seems distant even though his work is at hand on every side, I prefer the absence of answer.

Wintry silhouettes show the structural beauty of the trees. One shaped liked cupped hands raises long bony fingers in supplication, another lies low along the ground but thin whips rise vertically to create a woody rood-screen filtering the view. Ivy encases whatever it can. On the banks, trees arch and stretch towards the water, bowing into the greedy river, which may accept the sweep of a branch graciously but often becomes more demanding, teaming with its destructive ally wind for a subtle pull to loosen the grip of the shallow-rooted, spindly not-yet-trunks and take its prize.

Seasons change. This place is compelling in any weather, but summer brings burgeoning ferns to take over the valley, forging a veritable jungle, re-shaping the environment, cutting the trees down to size, obscuring views and modulating the tone of the river. The rocks remember their core identity, spreading a blanket of heat over the surface of the water. Water-boatmen mass in the calm water, flicking and twizzling like a gathering of Venetian gondoliers. Nearby buildings are lost from sight in the blossoming of nature, wild flowers dotting the intensity of green with bright splashes of colour, foxgloves, ragged robin, tansy and holy rope.

The sense of being enclosed and protected from outside interference, helps us to go within and reach inside for layers of thought unexploited under the glare of gaze and gossip, conditions of everyday life. Put a hand through the reflection and draw out the patterns from below. The dynamism of this place is a harmony of elements and proportions, of scale that generates intimacy. Its unusual atmosphere is created by that sense of containment and by an awareness of survival that sets it apart. It is a place for human silence and nature's eternal conversation. For those that seek it, an unfailing source of revitalizing energy.

The power of Mardoul does not spring from an historical event or special significance. It has no legends, no religious connection, no oral narrative, no role in song. It is not even obviously a place of the imagination, conjuring up mythic images or oozing menace. And yet it is numinous. So if this comes not from history or religion, great deeds or mystical events, what is the source? I believe it is the intrinsic spirit of place, made appreciable by the combination of elements, the harmonies of nature, the scale we can encompass, all uniting in this two hundred metre stretch of a small river in an ordinary valley. It is the amalgamation and the simplicity that provide the magic. Water smells of life, and the words of water tell us back our own stories.

In this hallowed space, a portal to the self swings open. In those watery words we can hear our own essential thoughts. Inside a containment of air, rock and river the harmony of physical being and spiritual need is easily felt. Boundaries dissolve. I am drawn in by the lure of the place's character, cleansing, affirmative, beguiling, profoundly pacific. It is the undercurrent, the pull below, the call to submission. Leave the other world behind. Mardoul's is an enlightened embrace, a sudden key to experiencing the true relation between movement and stillness in the heart. Sometimes the dividing line of life and landscape is thin.

BELONGING

Without a sense of belonging, we are lost. It may take a long search to find that essential connection to the land, many steps beyond the false assumption that where we begin is always the most potent root-bed for our spirit. It is natural to seek anchorage, but anchors do not root. They are pulled up for each new move and re-cast at the next destination. There may be a long quest for the special place because that feeling of belonging and rightness of context is often unexpected and to be found in unlikely places and relationships. So we may drag our cord of being through countless miles and over many seas before arriving at the place of true affinity with landscape.

For some the moment of arrival is never sought. For others, it never comes. Once there, we may leave and come back, or leave and be forever asunder from some inner sliver, lacking the last piece of the jigsaw of self. Then life is lived from the outside, looking at landscape like a postcard or photograph, always separate, never full engaged. It is the engagement with our natural geophysical context that can make us whole.

Belonging is not sentimental attachment. Our place may or may not be one of ease and comfort, but true connection with the land will be sustaining. We must mirror our inner landscape with the physical setting in which we fix our lives. Just as sailors separated from the sea lose a load-bearing wall of identity, so the loss of trees or stones or still water or cherished city skylines can be a fatal blow to happiness and the inner comfort of different individuals.

Instinct draws us to what we need in the natural world, the place in which a fundamental recognition, almost a remembered state, secures our natural rhythms and buoys us up against all the uncertainties of life. It can bring the reassurance of childhood, remembered places with familiar names and smells that trigger affirming memories. It may equally be a foreign land where a depth of affinity can take us by surprise.

Harmony with landscape enables our most positive self to thrive and operate at a level beyond daily necessities. The question 'Who am I?' is indistinguishable from 'Where am I?' Finding our right place ends all those separations from lost selves, scattered along the pathway of our lives. Arriving gathers them up again, they come flying in from all quarters, with the tender flight of homing pigeons. Being outside, inside our natural milieu brings completion. Then the world is ours and we can say 'I am home', holding the soft hand of the beloved.

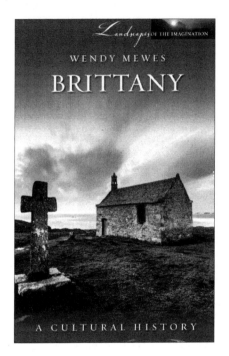

For an extract, see over...

Towns: Walls that bind

Quimper, capital of Finistère, is centred around the Odet and Steir rivers - the Breton name Kemper means confluence - its flowery passerelles a legacy of access for former large houses with private bridges to the medieval walled city. Although the earliest settlement was on the left bank at Locmaria, legendary founder King Gradlon began his capital on the opposite side of the river, where the luminously beautiful Gothic cathedral of Saint Corentin now stands. The old walled city preserves short stretches of its fortifications and many colourful half-timbered houses in the narrow streets, today transformed into smart shopping areas.

It's this blend of modernity and history-laden architecture that appeals to the tourist market, but in essence Quimper remains the rural haven of the bourgeoisie that has characterised its development since the Revolution. The town was surprised to find itself the departmental capital in 1791 when it was thought that the choice of commercial port Landerneau on the river Elorn in Léon was a done deal, and the effect of the political manoeuvring that led to this administrative accident has done little ultimately to change a leisurely, affable pace of urban life.

We get an immediate and detailed picture of post-Revolutionary Quimper from Watkin Tench (1758-1833), who served with Admiral Bligh in the British fleet blockading the French navy at Brest in 1794. They were captured and held first on a prison-ship at Brest before being transferred to Quimper in February 1795 under a loose house-arrest which permitted Tench to amble at will around the city and surrounding areas. He spoke fluent French (no more use to him 'than in Delhi' outside the town where only Breton was spoken) and recorded his observations of the situation in letters to a friend.

He describes how the 'stately elms' of a public walk along the river have been cut down to the chagrin of the population, to be sent to Brest for the urgent ship-building required by France's post-revolutionary wars. The streets of Quimper are narrow, winding and dirty, many with new politically correct names like Street of Voltaire and Liberty Square. Some fine large old houses exist, but all have been shorn of their heraldic emblems in the democratic zeal that prevailed during the Terror. This precaution has been applied in the smallest degree: in Tench's quarters 'I now eat with spoons whence the family marks are carefully expunged'.

Books by Wendy Mewes

Finistère: Things to see and do at the End of the World

Walking and other activities in Finistère

Discovering the History of Brittany

Guide to the Nantes-Brest Canal

Crossing Brittany (travelogue)

Walking the Brittany Coast (Vol 2, Morlaix to Benodet)

Footprint Guide to Brittany

Footprint Brittany West Coast

The Legends of Brittany

Brittany, a cultural history (Signal Books series Landscapes of the Imagination)

Huelgoat (short illustrated guide)

Monts d'Arrée (short illustrated guide)

Walks in Finistère

Fiction
Moon Garden
The Five of Cups
The Shape of Mist (short stories)